EMERSON
FITTIPALDI

By GORDON KIRBY

PHOTOGRAPHS BY

GARY GOLD

DAVID HUTSON

DAVID PHIPPS

MARC SPROULE

HAZLETON PUBLISHING

PUBLISHER
Richard Poulter

EXECUTIVE PUBLISHER
Elizabeth Le Breton

ART EDITOR
Steve Small

PRODUCTION MANAGER
George Greenfield

HOUSE EDITOR
Peter Lovering

PRODUCTION ASSISTANT
Deirdre Fenney

STATISTICS
John Taylor

Colour photography by:
Gary Gold – front and back covers, pages 72, 73 *(top)*, 76-77,
78 and 79
David Phipps – pages 65–71
David Hutson – pages 73 *(bottom)*, 74-75 and 76 *(left)*
Marc Sproule – page 80

Black and white photographs contributed by:
Autosport (Michael C. Brown), Gary Gold, David Hutson,
David Phipps and Marc Sproule.

This first edition published in 1990 by
Hazleton Publishing, 3 Richmond Hill, Richmond,
Surrey TW10 6RE.

ISBN: 0-905138-78-3

Printed in England by BAS Printers Ltd, Over Wallop,
Hampshire.

Typesetting by First Impression Graphics Ltd, Richmond,
Surrey.

DISTRIBUTORS

UK & OTHER MARKETS
Osprey Publishing Limited, 59 Grosvenor Street
London W1X 9DA

USA & CANADA
Motorbooks International, PO Box 2
729 Prospect Avenue, Osceola
Wisconsin 54020, USA

AUSTRALIA
Technical Book & Magazine Co. Pty
289-299 Swanston Street
Melbourne, Victoria 3000

Universal Motor Publications
c/o Automoto Motoring Bookshop
152-154 Clarence Street
Sydney 2000, New South Wales

NEW ZEALAND
David Bateman Limited, 'Golden Heights'
32-34 View Road, Glenfield, Auckland 10

OTHER TITLES IN THIS SERIES

Nigel Mansell

Niki Lauda

Alain Prost

Gilles Villeneuve

Jochen Rindt

PROLOGUE

To begin with it was almost a sad sight. A former two-times World Champion, the youngest man ever to win the title, in fact, roaming the American countryside with his new companion Teresa, trying to restart a broken career.

Emerson Fittipaldi had retired from motor racing at the end of 1980 after five debilitating years of trying to build and race his own Grand Prix cars. He kept his team going for two more seasons before retiring to Brazil, apparently gone from motor racing for ever and forgotten by the fickle world of Formula One. Then, in the spring of 1984, there was Fittipaldi in the USA, looking to go racing again, this time in Indycars.

Many people said he was doing it for the money. He was broke and missed the limelight, suggested the naysayers. He was trying, they said, to race again for the worst possible reasons. With these motivations, went the theory, Fittipaldi was doomed to failure, maybe even grievous injury.

The man himself grinned and shook his head at these suggestions. 'No, no,' he said as he wandered the paddock at the first Long Beach GP for Indycars. 'I want to enjoy racing again as a sport. I hated those last years in Formula One. For me, it was a terrible time. Now I am ready to try to go racing again for the enjoyment. If success and money follow, it will be fantastic, but I want to enjoy the sport again. I miss it, you know: the sensations of driving a fast racing car and the competition. I've been racing go-karts in Brazil and all I can tell you is I want to enjoy the feel of driving again a racing car.'

So there he was, rumpled driving suit stuffed in his bag, Teresa at his side. Could he start again from the bottom and climb all the way back to the top? Few people believed it. Most thought he was a sad case, trying to recapture his lost youth.

Yet the following summer he would win his first Indycar race and five years later he stood on the podium at Indianapolis, an emotional winner in one of the most spectacular finishes to the 500 in recent history. Later in the year, after winning four more races, Fittipaldi was crowned CART's PPG Indycar World Series Champion, and in November the official announcement came that in 1990 he would join Penske Racing, America's most famous and successful racing team.

In many ways, Fittipaldi's rebirth as an Indycar driver mirrored his meteoric rise 15 years earlier to Formula One stardom. He arrived in Europe in 1969, the 22-year-old son of a Brazilian motor racing journalist and radio commentator. Emerson started his European career in Formula Ford but by mid-season he was winning Formula Three races, and the following year he was a works Lotus Formula Two driver.

In July 1970 Emerson made his F1 debut for Team Lotus and in October he won the United States GP at Watkins Glen, only his fourth F1 start! Two years later, a few months before his 26th birthday, Fittipaldi won the World Championship. He thus became the youngest man ever to do so, a record that remains unbroken to this day.

Encouraged by his father, Fittipaldi started racing as a teenager, first on a 50 cc motor cycle, then in go-karts. By the time he was 17, the legal minimum age in Brazil at the time to apply for a driving licence, Emerson started to race cars. His first outing was in a friend's road-going Renault, which he proceeded to crash.

Nevertheless, he kept at it, driving whatever he could get his hands on. In 1967 Fittipaldi won both the Brazilian go-kart championship and the national Formula Vee title. The FVee championship came aboard a car bearing his own name, built by Emerson and older brother Wilson, who was also a competitive racing driver.

By the end of 1968 Emerson realised he had achieved as much as possible in Brazil. If he wanted to progress and become a professional Formula One driver he had to go to Europe. He considered trying to race in F3 in Italy but was convinced by Jerry Cunningham, a Brazilian-based Englishman, that he should go to England and try his hand at a new 'low cost' type of single-seater racing called Formula Ford. So it was that Fittipaldi set the stage not only for his own burgeoning career but also for a long list of South American drivers who have subsequently made their marks in international motor racing.

Above: *Posing in front of the family garage with older brother Wilson. The two brothers raced and built karts and cars together before going to Europe. This was ten years before their abortive attempt to build a successful Brazilian F1 car.*

Right: *Hanging it out in enthusiastic style in a borrowed, road-going Renault.*

Emerson arrived in England in March 1969. He purchased a state-of-the-art Merlyn Mk 11A chassis and, with the help of engine builder Dennis Rowland, began his European adventure. Fittipaldi prepared the Merlyn on his own and raced the car without a mechanic or team behind him, something that Emerson himself admits would not be possible today.

His first race in Europe was at Zandvoort in Holland. He qualified second fastest and led his qualifying heat before blowing his engine. Next came a race at Snetterton and this time Fittipaldi started from pole position, setting fastest lap on his way to victory.

Emerson followed up this first European win with a series of good results, including third place at the Chimay road circuit in Belgium, second at Vallelunga in Italy, and another win at Oulton Park. He then returned to Norfolk, beating all the hotshoes of the time like Tony Trimmer, Ray Allen and Dave Walker.

By this time Fittipaldi reckoned he was ready to make the break into Formula Three, and he was able to strike a deal to buy a new Lotus 59 and run the car in the colours of Jim Russell's fledgling racing drivers' school. Emerson sold his FF Merlyn and put everything into running his new machine.

For the move up to F3, Fittipaldi enjoyed a mechanic – no less a man than Ralph Firman, who went on to achieve worldwide renown as the founder of Van Diemen, generally acknowledged as history's most successful Formula Ford marque. Emerson put in a full seven days' testing with his Lotus prior to his first race and went on to win eight of the eleven F3 races he started that summer. By the end of the year he was considered the hottest up-and-comer in Europe, and for 1970 he was hired by Colin Chapman to drive in his works Lotus F2 team.

'Without a doubt, that was the most important stage in my racing career,' comments Fittipaldi. 'The timing and sequence of events couldn't have been better for me. It was because of good luck and people like Jim Russell and Ralph Firman. All the ingredients were right, the timing was perfect and luck was on my side.'

Nor did it take much longer for Emerson to make the move from F2 to F1. The Lotus F2 cars weren't the best but Fittipaldi's feel for the car and his ability to work with the mechanics and team were reported to Colin Chapman. Early in the year Chapman decided he should give the young Brazilian a run in one of his F1 cars.

'I remember someone from Lotus said, "Mr Chapman wants to talk to you,"' recalls Emerson. 'I walked into his office and he was sitting at his desk and I was shaking! I was saying to myself, "He's going to ask me to drive one of his Formula One cars." That was such an important moment in my career and I will never forget it.

'I remember Colin invited me to join the team and I remember refusing to go to the first race because I felt I didn't have enough experience. I felt I needed more experience in Formula Two. Colin wanted me to start at the Dutch GP in June but I wanted to wait another month or two.'

Jochen Rindt was Chapman's number one driver that year. The team produced the wedge-shaped Lotus 72 to replace the ageing 49 but Rindt was never very enamoured with the new car. Ultimately the Austrian won that year's World Championship, although he was awarded the title posthumously after crashing to his death in a 72 during practice for the Italian GP.

Rindt started his run to the championship with a last-lap victory at Monaco aboard one of the old 49s. Later in the year he won four races in a row and it was during this stretch, as Rindt rather reluctantly took over one of the new 72s, that Fittipaldi made his Grand Prix debut as Chapman's third driver.

His first F1 race was in a Lotus 49 at Brands Hatch where he finished a steady eighth. Two weeks later Fittipaldi took his first World Championship points, coming home a strong fourth in the German GP. At the next race, in Austria, he again ran with the leaders before running out of fuel. Chapman's third-string driver was beginning to make his presence felt.

At Monza two weeks later, however, Rindt was killed when a front brakeshaft broke, and Team Lotus withdrew from the race. The team missed the next race in Canada but was back for the United States GP at Watkins Glen with Fittipaldi backing up Swede Reine Wisell.

Emerson qualified third at the Glen but made a poor start. However, he moved up steadily and, towards the end of the race, leader Jackie Stewart hit trouble. So too did Pedro Rodriguez, who had to stop for fuel while leading, and suddenly there was Fittipaldi in the lead! In only his fourth F1 race he was a winner, giving the dispirited Lotus team exactly the shot in the arm it needed.

Emerson and Maria-Helena enjoy the champagne after he had won his first F1 race at Watkins Glen in October 1970.

Early in the 1970 United States GP, Fittipaldi chases the leaders, staying clear of Graham Hill in Rob Walker's Lotus 72, Gold Leaf Team Lotus team-mate Reine Wisell and a string of others.

For the '71 season Fittipaldi became Lotus's number one driver alongside Wisell. Changes in tyre design meant most of the year was spent adapting the Lotus 72 to the new rubber, however. Also, Fittipaldi was forced to miss the Dutch GP after breaking his sternum in a road accident while driving home to Switzerland from Monaco.

As the year wore on Team Lotus became more and more competitive, with Emerson taking a pair of thirds at Paul Ricard and Silverstone. At the Österreichring in August he was able to chase poleman Jo Siffert's BRM home to a close second, only four seconds behind at the chequered flag. Fittipaldi finished sixth in that year's World Championship and Team Lotus's hopes for 1972 were high.

'We had a very tough year in 1971,' explains Fittipaldi, 'because there was a big change in the tyres. In 1970 there was still a little bit of tread in the tyres but in 1971 the tyres were completely slick for the first time. The slicks generated so much more grip that the 72's suspension wasn't strong enough.

'We had problems with bump steer and toe-in under power, and under braking the tyres would toe-out. The whole suspension was moving. It took us about six months to get the car working but by the end of the season the car was really beautiful.'

Fittipaldi had to miss the '71 Dutch Grand Prix after breaking his sternum in a road accident following the Monaco GP. He returned to action in France, finishing a strong third behind the Tyrrells of Jackie Stewart and François Cevert.

Second at the Österreichring in 1971 was Emerson's best result in his first full year in Formula One.

*Emerson won the first of five Grands Prix in 1972 in Spain,
paving the way to his first World Championship at a
mere 25 years of age. Here he leads Lotus team-mate
Dave Walker.*

For 1972 there was a change to the colours of Team Lotus. Gone were the red, white and gold of the Imperial Tobacco Company's Gold Leaf cigarette brand in exchange for the gold-trimmed black of the John Player Special brand.

For Fittipaldi, the new year was one he would not easily forget. He won five Grands Prix – Spain, Belgium, Britain, Austria and Italy – and four other non-championship F1 races. In doing so he beat Jackie Stewart and Denny Hulme to the World Championship, establishing himself at 25 years and nine months as the youngest man ever to win the title.

'That was a fantastic year,' recalls Emerson. 'The car was competitive everywhere we raced and I usually qualified in the first two rows. The car was very reliable as well and we won the championship because of our finishing record just as much as being able to drive fast. It's like any time you win a championship, it was a real team effort.

'And you know,' he adds with a faraway grin, 'it was a great pleasure to win the championship by winning the race at Monza. I remember the feeling on the victory lap that day. It was just fantastic!'

*With Maria-Helena in 1972 on the way to his first World
Championship. Carefree days…*

Left: *Lotus founder Colin Chapman leans into the cockpit
to listen to Emerson's impressions of the Lotus 72 during the
summer of 1972.*

Emerson chalks up his third win of the year at Brands Hatch in '72. Chapman is over the pit wall with his hat in the air, doing a victory jig.

Emerson fought hard to win the '72 Austrian GP, holding off Denny Hulme's McLaren by just over a second.

On the podium in Austria in '72 after his fourth win of the year. Four weeks later at Monza, he was World Champion.

The 1973 season brought Emerson a new team-mate in Ronnie Peterson. Like Fittipaldi, the tall, blond Swede had made his Grand Prix debut in 1970. Driving for the new March team, Peterson soon became the King of Formula Two, winning the F2 championship in '71. He also finished second to Jackie Stewart in that year's World Championship, although he wasn't able to win a race.

Peterson stayed with March in 1972 but had a terrible year with a series of experimental cars. Through all this Ronnie continued to demonstrate tremendous flair behind the wheel and at the end of the year Colin Chapman signed him to partner Fittipaldi in '73.

For Emerson, the new year started in high gear. He won three of the first four races and looked ready to defend his World Championship. Meanwhile Peterson was proving just how fast he was, rarely qualifying outside the front row and taking no fewer than nine pole positions during the year. There was no question that Colin Chapman had one of the finest driver pairings in the history of Grand Prix racing.

*Emerson continued his fine start to the '73 season in Brazil,
leading from the first corner to score one of the easiest wins
of his career. Cevert, so impressive in Argentina, follows
(below). At the finish the delight of Colin Chapman
(right) was surpassed only by the joy of the fans, who
bore the local hero away in triumph.*

*Spain, 1973 and Fittipaldi's third GP win from the first
four races of the year. At that stage of the season the
defending champion looked good, but things soon began
to go wrong.*

As far as the World Championship was concerned, however, it began to go wrong in mid-season. At the Dutch GP, Fittipaldi crashed in practice when a wheel came apart. For a few minutes he was trapped in the car and, although he drove in the race, Emerson's left ankle was injured. Some ligaments were torn and the injury put a damper on the rest of his season.

In September at Monza, the very place he'd wrapped up the World Championship 12 months earlier, Fittipaldi had to cede his title to Jackie Stewart. Bitter-sweet it was, as well, because Emerson finished a close second to team-mate Peterson in Italy, with Stewart fourth after a pit stop.

'Ronnie was a great team-mate,' says Emerson of their year together at Lotus in '73. 'I enjoyed every minute of working with Ronnie. He was one of the best friends I ever had in racing. And, of course, we had some fantastic races together, really fantastic.

'I think for me the Brazilian Grand Prix at the beginning of 1973 was the best race we had. He was on pole and I started second and at the start of the race Ronnie took the lead. I was chasing, trying very hard to pass him.

'I think one of the best passes I ever made in my life was in that race. Going into the third turn at Interlagos, which was a banked corner, I decided to give everything to pass him. Ronnie saw me coming and went down low and I passed him on the outside. I took the lead and won the race. That was an incredible dice.

'Another good dice we had was at the French GP. Jody Scheckter took the lead and Denny Hulme and myself were chasing, trying to pass, but we couldn't do it. Ronnie was right behind and at half-distance I decided to let Ronnie pass me and see if he could pass Jody. So I waved Ronnie by and he started attacking Jody.

'But Ronnie couldn't find a way by Jody so after a while I decided to try again. I passed Ronnie and started attacking Jody; by then it was getting to the end of the race and I was desperate to pass. Then we touched going into the hairpin and Jody and I were out of the race.

'I bent my front suspension and Jody bent his rear suspension. So Ronnie won. It was actually his first Grand Prix win and after the race he came up to me and said, "Thanks, Emerson. You did a great job!" He was a fantastic guy, a great friend and team-mate.'

Nevertheless, Fittipaldi decided near the end of the year to leave Lotus and Peterson. In the closing months of 1973 he was wooed heavily by Marlboro, who were planning a move for '74 from BRM to McLaren. Marlboro had come into Formula One with BRM in 1972 but the cigarette giant decided that the best chance for long-term success lay with McLaren, and Fittipaldi was the man they wanted to lead the team.

*In serious conversation with Ed Alexander, Goodyear's
racing boss of the time, and Bert Baldwin, the tyre
company's chief field engineer.*

'For me it was a very difficult decision, for sure,' says Fittipaldi. 'Lotus was a great team and I felt very much at home there, like it was a family. But Marlboro is a huge company and there was no doubt in my mind that they were very serious about winning Grand Prix races. And, of course, McLaren had been very competitive in Formula One. I had some of my toughest races in 1973 against the McLarens and, finally, I decided it was the way to go.'

Brazil, '74 and Emerson has changed teams. Here his Marlboro McLaren chases former team-mate Peterson's JPS Lotus. Peterson hit trouble and Emerson won, setting the stage for his second world title.

The split with Lotus, the marque which had had so much to do with Emerson's early career, left a bad taste in Colin Chapman's mouth. An imperious man who preferred to be in control of 'the deal', he felt he had been underhanded by Marlboro and Fittipaldi.

'Colin was more than just a team manager,' Emerson recalls with genuine affection. 'He introduced so many things to Formula One. He was a master of the technical aspects of Formula One and there is no question that he helped my career a lot. For me, he was like a teacher or a tutor. Going through the problems you normally face with any Formula One car with Colin behind me was just fantastic. For sure he was a genius. He could be very difficult to work with sometimes but he knew a lot about motor racing and racing cars, more than anybody I ever worked with.'

The move to McLaren gave Fittipaldi a chance to apply much of what he had learned at Lotus to his new team. McLaren's M23 had first appeared at the beginning of the previous season and before the year was out the car had won three races in the hands of Denny Hulme and Peter Revson. Designed by Gordon Coppuck, the M23 would keep Fittipaldi in the thick of the hunt for the championship in 1974.

Second place behind Jody Scheckter's Tyrrell in the '74 British GP at Brands Hatch kept Emerson in the thick of the battle for the championship.

Right: *Mosport Park, Canada in September 1974.*
Fittipaldi beat championship rival Clay Regazzoni's
Ferrari by 13 seconds. With one race to go, the two were
equal on points.

Goodyear engineer Baldwin and Emerson in a more relaxed
moment. McLaren boss Teddy Mayer communes with his
clipboard, trying to figure out the right set-up.

Indeed, Emerson won three races that year – Brazil, Belgium and Canada. He also had pairs of second, third and fourth places and eked out the championship by three points from Ferrari driver Clay Regazzoni. Two championships in three years meant Fittipaldi was at the apogee of Grand Prix racing, and he was even selected for the first time as the year's number one driver by the editor of *Autocourse*!

On the podium at Mosport Park in '74 with Regazzoni
(left) and third-placed Peterson.

*Defending champion once again in '75 – and on the leading
edge of eyeglass fashion as well.*

The following year started well enough with a win in Argentina and a close second to countryman Carlos Pace in Brazil. In South Africa, Fittipaldi hit electrical trouble early in the race and after repairs ran to the finish, many laps behind. Then came a disastrous Spanish GP in Barcelona.

Serious shortcomings with the guard rail around the street circuit caused a drivers' strike during practice. Much of the guard railing was loosely bolted to the retaining posts. Some of the guard rail was simply laid in place without any bolts at all! Practice was delayed and most drivers threatened to boycott the weekend. In the end all but Fittipaldi practised and raced. Emerson stuck by his decision not to drive and, after three slow practice laps with his hand in the air, he withdrew.

*On the podium with Maria-Helena and Teddy Mayer at
Silverstone in '75. His victory in the rain-shortened British
GP was the last of Fittipaldi's 14 Grand Prix wins.*

His decision drew a lot of fire from fans and the press but, to this day, Emerson remains convinced of his position. 'I have no doubts that what I did was correct in the circumstances,' he reflects. 'I believed then and I still believe that the organisers of that race were completely irresponsible. It was a very difficult weekend for me, very difficult. Particularly when none of the other drivers supported me.'

The race took place without the World Champion and ended in woeful misery. Leader Rolf Stommelen crashed heavily, his car leaping the guard rail, tearing down some catch-fencing and coming to rest in a restricted area. Unfortunately some spectators were watching from the restricted zone and Stommelen's car killed three of them and a photographer. Stommelen was taken to hospital with two broken legs, a broken wrist and cracked ribs.

At Monaco a few weeks later Fittipaldi chased hard after Niki Lauda to finish three seconds behind the Austrian's winning Ferrari. At that point, Emerson still led the championship but, apart from winning at Silverstone in July, the rest of the season was a catalogue of disasters. In the end Lauda beat him soundly to the championship and that somewhat lucky win in the rain-shortened British GP would turn out to be the last of Emerson's 14 Grand Prix victories. At the end of the previous year he had taken the decision to start his own Formula One team in partnership with his brother Wilson...

Says Emerson of his two years with McLaren: 'Working with the McLaren team and Teddy Mayer was really something because that was a great team. The M23 was a really quick car and we were very competitive in 1974. But the McLaren was not as good as the Lotus 72 had been from track to track.

'At some tracks the M23 didn't work and we had to work like crazy to improve the car to make it acceptable and be competitive. But there were a lot of good relationships and good team work at McLaren. I enjoyed it a lot and it was a great experience. When I look back on it, I realise that leaving Marlboro and McLaren was one of the biggest mistakes I ever made in my life.'

Left: *Driving his own Copersucar Fittipaldi in 1976,
Emerson had a tough year. He finished the season with three
points from a trio of sixths.*

*In the pits in 1978 with Kiwi engineer Ralph Bellamy. The
struggle to be competitive was only getting tougher.*

Nevertheless, at the time Emerson was full of enthusiasm for his new project. With sponsorship from Brazilian sugar producer Copersucar, the Fittipaldi brothers leaped into the job of building and producing their own Grand Prix contender. Wilson drove the first Fittipaldi F1 car in 1975 and for the '76 season Emerson stepped into the driver's seat, with Wilson managing the operation. As hard as they worked, however, the project never really came together. Emerson stood on the podium at a Grand Prix only twice more, finishing second in Brazil in 1978 and third at Long Beach in 1980.

'I underestimated what it would take to build our own team, particularly with the cost and technology in Formula One escalating so rapidly,' says Emerson. 'I never thought it would be as difficult as it was. We were just unable to generate the financial and technical support we expected from Brazil. It was very disappointing. But when you have a bad experience you learn some lessons and, in this case, I learned many lessons.

*Fourth place in Argentina's '77 season-opener gave the
Fittipaldi brothers reason for hope in Emerson's second year
with the team.*

*On the victory lap at Long Beach, 1980 after finishing third
to Nelson Piquet and Riccardo Patrese. It was Piquet's
first Grand Prix win – and Emerson's last visit to the
podium in F1.*

'The first few years weren't really a big problem, even though the cars were bad. Then in 1978 I had a good year, including a second in the Brazilian Grand Prix. The car was fast that year and I was enjoying driving. But in 1979 and '80 the cars were a disaster and I did not enjoy myself at all.

'Those two years were my last in Formula One and I was going to the races only because it was an obligation. I was too involved in the problems of trying to make the team work and I neglected my marriage and my personal life. For me, it was a very, very bad time in my life.'

By the end of 1980, with his marriage of ten years to Maria-Helena coming apart, Fittipaldi retired. For two years he kept his team going but his cars were always at the back of the field and often non-qualifiers. At the end of 1982, Emerson turned his back on Formula One for good and returned home to Brazil. There, he put his time and energy into running the family orange-growing and automobile accessory businesses.

*Left: Kitted out in Copersucar colours and with breathing
gear in 1978.*

*Long Beach GP, 1984. The first year for CART and
Indycars on the streets of the California city was also the
occasion of Fittipaldi's Indycar debut. Aboard Pepe
Romero's pink year-old March he finished fifth.*

'After I stopped racing in Formula One, I didn't miss driving a racing car for a couple of years,' says Fittipaldi. 'Those last few years in Formula One were so unhappy that I didn't miss driving at all, until after we closed down the team. But in 1983 I started racing superkarts with some friends in Brazil and that got me excited again about driving racing cars.'

Emerson won a number of kart races and even a championship in '83. As the year wore on he began to think more and more about going racing again. And at the end of that year Ralph Sanchez called Fittipaldi with the suggestion that Emerson drive in the upcoming Miami GP IMSA race. Sanchez lives in Miami and was working at the time on creating a street race for IMSA GTP cars in the downtown area of the city. He reckoned Fittipaldi was just the personality he needed to help give the race a good kick-off.

Emerson decided to accept Sanchez's offer and in February 1984 he made his motor racing comeback aboard a Chevrolet-powered March GTP car. He qualified on the pole, led the race and realised that racing was still the most important thing in his life.

'While I was in Miami, Pepe Romero asked me if I wanted to go to Indianapolis with him. He told me he was buying an Indycar and putting together a team and he wanted me to drive. This was perfect timing because I was excited and motivated to drive again and Indycars were exactly the thing to bring me back.'

Back in 1974, Fittipaldi had tested a McLaren Indycar at Indianapolis. At the time he didn't think much of the experience, believing that the cars were very dangerous. In the intervening ten years, however, many changes had taken place in the design and crash-resistance of Indycars, and the more Emerson thought about this new prospect, the more determined he was to do it.

The gravel-voiced Romero bought a year-old March-Cosworth and at the end of March his little team set off for California and the Long Beach GP. That was the first year Indycars replaced F1 on the streets of the California city and there on the grid for that inaugural CART race was Romero's pink March with E. Fittipaldi at the wheel.

With wife-to-be Teresa at his side, Emerson had a good weekend in California. He qualified in midfield and ran well in the race, finishing fifth, two laps behind winner Mario Andretti. Two weeks later Fittipaldi had his first taste of racing a single-seater on an oval, coming home a distant twelfth in a 200-mile race on the one-mile Phoenix Raceway oval.

'That was fantastic!' he enthused after the race. 'No matter how much experience you might have in a Grand Prix car, it can never prepare you for this. I have never experienced so much wheel-to-wheel racing in my life! But I tell you, this is what gives

*In the pits at Indianapolis in 1984. With Romero's small,
inexperienced team, Emerson's first month of May was a
difficult baptism.*

me the motivation to come back. There is so much to learn, so many new things.'

Next came Indianapolis and for this race Romero bought a new car. But the job of preparing and running a car effectively at the giant superspeedway in the heart of America's Midwest proved too much for Romero's little team. Fittipaldi was able to qualify for the 500 but was an early retirement after an oil-line fell off.

By then, Emerson realised that he was taking his life in his hands with Romero's operation and he sensibly decided to back away from the team. He missed the next two races and then found work for a pair of races with another small team. At The Meadowlands Emerson impressed in the rain and finished the race, but he knew there was no future in struggling around in such uncompetitive machinery.

Fittipaldi's big break in Indycars came in August in the typically hard-edged way of motor racing. At the Michigan 500, up-and-coming youngster Chip Ganassi had a terrible, high-speed accident with Al Unser Jnr. Ganassi's car flipped and came down on top of the guard rail, knocking the young driver unconscious. Although he survived, ultimately returning to the sport as a team owner after trying his hand in a few races, Ganassi was out of action for the rest of the year. Ganassi had driven for Patrick Racing, one of Indycar racing's top teams, and the carpet-bagging Fittipaldi was the man selected to replace him.

In his first race for Patrick, the Brazilian finished a workmanlike fourth and at the end of the season team owner Pat Patrick decided Fittipaldi would drive for him on a regular basis in 1985. Patrick's team leader was Indycar veteran Gordon Johncock, who had

*In four of the last six races of 1984, Emerson subbed in
Patrick Racing's second car for the injured Chip Ganassi.
Here he motors around the Caesar's Palace parking lot in
Las Vegas.*

Left: *Testing the latest March 85C at Laguna Seca in February '85. March major-domo Robin Herd chats with Patrick men George Huening, Jim McGee and Peter Gibbons as Emerson awaits their next move.*

won the Indy 500 for Patrick in 1973 and '82. The combination of oval track ace Johncock and former F1 champion Fittipaldi seemed ideal for CART's demanding mixture of road and oval races.

Fittipaldi started the '85 season in good form with a distant but clean run to second place at Long Beach. Then at Indianapolis Johncock decided on the eve of qualifying to retire from racing and Fittipaldi suddenly found himself as Patrick's team leader. He responded in kind, qualifying fifth for the 500 and running with the leaders in the race. For a while he looked like finishing among the first three or four but late in the race Emerson's oil tank failed.

By now it was clear that Fittipaldi had established himself as an Indycar driver. He followed up his performance at Indianapolis with third place at Portland and second at The Meadowlands. Then in July's Michigan 500, helped by a typically high rate of attrition, Emerson came through to score his first Indycar victory.

At Long Beach in '85, Fittipaldi was back in business as a regular driver for Patrick in all races. Here he leads Roberto Guerrero on his way to second behind Mario Andretti.

By June 1985 Fittipaldi was Patrick's team leader after
Gordon Johncock had decided to retire before qualifying at
Indianapolis. Nevertheless, Emerson still had some things
to learn about ovals, finishing eighth at Milwaukee the
week after the Indy 500.

'For sure this is a fantastic moment for me,' he said after the race. 'We may not have been the fastest car today, but the car ran really well and the team did a great job in the pits. I was able to race with some of the leaders and I am learning more and more about competing with the top Indycar drivers. Today, I feel for the first time as if I am a real Indycar driver.'

He had little luck in the second half of the season but accumulated enough points to finish sixth in CART's PPG Cup championship. In two years Fittipaldi had already come a long way but there was much more to follow. For the '86 season his new career in Indycars was given a big boost by the arrival of a new sponsor – Marlboro.

Emerson has three children from his first marriage and a daughter by second wife Teresa. Son Jayson was 13 when this photograph of papa Emerson was taken in 1986.

Above left: In the pits during the 1985 Pocono 500 on his way to sixth place. The bumpy old superspeedway in eastern Pennsylvania was finally abandoned by CART in 1989.

Emerson was third at the Portland International Raceway road course (left) in Oregon in 1985 behind Mario Andretti and Al Unser Jnr, one of four visits he made to the podium that year.

*Passing Gary Bettenhausen's similar March 86C on the
front straight at the Phoenix International Raceway oval
in 1986.*

*Contemplating his car's set-up in the pits in 1986. This
year saw the beginning of Fittipaldi's revived relationship
with sponsor Marlboro.*

*Working hard at the top of The Corkscrew at Laguna Seca
in 1986.*

Philip Morris's leading cigarette brand had a brief dalliance with Indycar racing in 1970, sponsoring the championship itself, which was then operated by CART's forerunner USAC. Conflicts with other cigarette manufacturers and USAC's lackadaisical attitude meant that Marlboro quickly withdrew from the series, however, moving instead in a major way into European racing and Formula One.

But by the mid-Eighties Marlboro recognised CART's efforts to market Indycar racing more aggressively. Philip Morris USA began looking for the right driver and team to sponsor, and Fittipaldi, with his successful Marlboro connections from 1974 and '75, was the logical choice. A deal was struck near the end of 1985 and for the '86 season there was Fittipaldi back in Marlboro's red and white colours.

On the face of it the new season wasn't any more successful than '85. Emerson finished seventh in the championship and scored one win in the rain at the Road America road circuit. But he was also on the pole for two road races – Portland and Toronto. Those were Emerson's first poles in Indycars and demonstrated that he was still making steady progress on the comeback trail.

The biggest shortcoming he had to contend with was reliability, finishing only eight of seventeen races. Few Indycar teams are capable of running more than one car but Patrick Racing was one of those which tried to field two. Kevin Cogan was Fittipaldi's team-mate and, indeed, Cogan won the year's season-opener on the Phoenix oval, finished a close second to Bobby Rahal at Indianapolis and beat Emerson into sixth place in CART's PPG Cup championship.

Patrick continued with Fittipaldi and Cogan in 1987. For the first time the team enjoyed the use of Ilmor Engineering's Chevrolet Indy V8 but, despite Emerson winning back-to-back road races in mid-summer at Cleveland and Toronto, the season as a whole was less successful than the previous year. Reliability was still a problem and drivers and team really struggled to find the right set-up in most oval races.

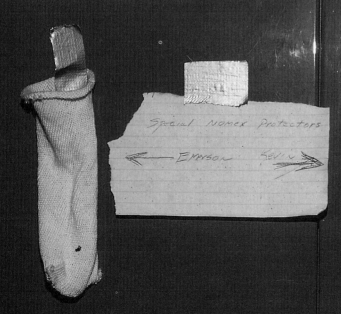

FITTIPALDI

COGAN

Special Nomex Protectors

← EMERSON   KEVIN →

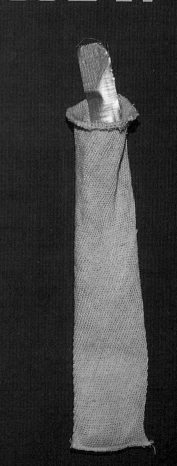

Above: *Fittipaldi's delighted pit crew celebrate his Toronto victory.*

Emerson was hot in July '87, winning two races in a row at Cleveland's Burke Lakefront Airport and Toronto's Exhibition Place. Left: Early in that year's Toronto race he leads Mario Andretti and Al Unser Jnr.

*Teresa attends most races and has become famous in her own
right, selling 'lucky' jewellery to other racing wives
and friends.*

*At home in Miami in '86, Emerson poses with his
Mercruiser powerboat and March Indycar.*

Below left: *Fittipaldi made his Grand Prix debut at the British GP in the summer of 1970. He was already letting his hair grow and sporting long 'muttonchop' sideburns.*

Below right: *The first of Emerson's 14 Grand Prix wins came in only his fourth race, the United States GP at Watkins Glen in October 1970.*

The 1971 season was tough. Tyre development hampered the Lotus 72 for much of the year, preventing Fittipaldi from winning a race. After missing the Dutch GP because of a road accident, he returned to action at the French GP, where he took third place behind the Tyrrells of Jackie Stewart and François Cevert.

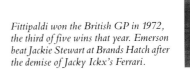

Fittipaldi won the British GP in 1972, the third of five wins that year. Emerson beat Jackie Stewart at Brands Hatch after the demise of Jacky Ickx's Ferrari.

On the way to his first World Championship in 1972 in the colours of John Player Special, Fittipaldi scored his fourth win of the year in the Austrian GP. Here he leads Clay Regazzoni's Ferrari and Denny Hulme's McLaren, the latter ultimately taking second place.

Overleaf: Emerson's third and last Grand Prix win of 1973 came at Montjuich Park, Spain in April after new team-mate Ronnie Peterson dropped out. This was also Fittipaldi's last GP victory for Team Lotus.

Left: *Moving from Lotus to McLaren for 1974,*
Fittipaldi narrowly beat Ferrari's Clay Regazzoni to
the world title. In the Canadian GP at Mosport Park
in September he scored his third win of the year,
finishing 13 seconds ahead of his championship rival.

The high point of Fittipaldi's last year as a Formula
One driver in 1980 was a good run to third place at
Long Beach in one of his own cars.

Opposite: *Emerson started the '75 season in style,*
winning in Argentina, but his year went steadily
downhill thereafter.

Fittipaldi found regular work in Indycars for 1985 with Pat Patrick's team. At Indianapolis in May he assumed the mantle of team leader after Gordon Johncock announced his retirement. In July's Michigan 500, Emerson scored his first Indycar victory.

In the closing months of 1984 Fittipaldi was hired by Pat Patrick to replace the injured Chip Ganassi. It was the opportunity which completed Emerson's rebirth as a racing driver.

For the '86 season Emerson continued with Patrick Racing and was reunited with sponsor Marlboro. He's pictured here in action at CART's season-closing race in Miami, his adopted American home town.

Overleaf: Patrick Racing switched from Cosworth to Chevrolet engines for 1987 and Emerson won two races. Steadily, the team was putting together a championship-winning package.

On the victory rostrum at the Cleveland airport circuit in 1987 with son Jayson. This was Fittipaldi's first win for Chevrolet.

After changing midway through the 1988 season from March to Lola chassis, Emerson was competitive everywhere. He scored his first win that year in changeable weather conditions at the Mid-Ohio road course in September.

Equipped with a Penske PC18, Fittipaldi dominated
much of the 1989 Indianapolis 500, although he had to
deal with a tremendous late-race challenge from
Al Unser Jnr before scoring the greatest single victory of his
long career.

Emerson took the 1989 CART/PPG Cup title at the
tiny Nazareth oval in September, where he scored his
fifth win of the year after a fierce duel with Rick Mears.

*Fittipaldi joined Penske Racing with sponsor Marlboro
for 1990. Here he leads his new team-mate Danny
Sullivan at the Portland, Oregon road course in June.*

For the '88 season, Patrick scaled back its operation to a single car for Fittipaldi. New to the team that year was engineer Morris Nunn, who had moved from F1 to Indycars at the end of 1984. Nunn had years of experience of building his own Ensign F1 cars, always on a shoestring budget. In Indycars he had worked successfully with Mario Andretti and Roberto Guerrero and his move to Patrick Racing had an immediately beneficial effect on the team's competitiveness.

Fittipaldi started the '88 season aboard a March–Chevrolet but March's 88C was a very difficult car to get the most out of. Patrick had been a loyal March customer since 1984 but, like most other teams, its patience with the Bicester marque's apparent indifference to its fading competitiveness in Indycar racing was wearing thin.

Early in the year Patrick bought a year-old Lola T87/00 but the car remained an unused spare through the first three months of the season. Aboard the unloved March 88C – which he referred to as 'The Wild Beast' – Emerson finished a lucky and distant second at Indianapolis. Finally, in July, the team decided to put aside its March and concentrate on racing the Lola.

Fittipaldi was immediately a much happier man and a more competitive driver. 'The Lola is so much better than the March!' he enthused. 'The car feels really good and it responds in the correct way to changes. With this car we will soon be winning races.'

Sure enough, he qualified on the pole at The Meadowlands at the end of July and dominated the first half of the race. A full-course yellow flag closed up the field, however, and on the restart Emerson found himself under heavy pressure from Al Unser Jnr. On fresh tyres, he got into the left-hander at the end of the back straight a little too hot and ran wide. On the exit from the corner Unser got up beside him, claiming the inside line for the chicane that followed.

Refusing to admit defeat, Fittipaldi tried to take his normal line into the chicane, only to bang wheels with Unser and bounce into the wall. Emerson's race was over and he scrambled from the car and shook his fist at Unser when the youngster came round again. Livid with rage, he stormed out of the track, his Latin temperament at full boil.

At the next race Emerson and Al Jnr met face to face and discussed their incident. Fittipaldi continued not to accept blame for the accident, although he was happy with Unser's open attitude and agreed to bury any bad feelings.

'I still think he was wrong in what he did,' commented Emerson at the time. 'But he was willing to talk and any time two racing drivers can have that kind of relationship, it is a good thing.'

Overleaf: Aboard this unloved March 88C ('The Wild Beast') Emerson was a distant and rather lucky second in the 1988 Indianapolis 500. He didn't enjoy that year's March at all, finding the car's handling to be unpredictably spooky.

*In July '88 the Patrick team finally replaced its pair of
Marches with a single Lola T87/00. Emerson won two
races after making the switch, but at Laguna Seca he was
eliminated by gearbox problems.*

A month later Emerson scored a pair of back-to-back victories at the Mid-Ohio and Road America road courses. At Mid-Ohio he made a superb pass for the lead, outbraking Mario Andretti on the *outside* at the end of the circuit's back straight. At Road America, where fuel mileage is always a major consideration, he judged it perfectly, allowing a comfortable mid-race cushion to dwindle to a lead of just one second over Bobby Rahal at the finish.

'After we changed to the Lola chassis we were very competitive on all types of tracks – road courses, short ovals and superspeedways,' commented Emerson at the end of 1988. 'With a year-old chassis we were competitive everywhere and that showed the potential of the team. The team has really improved over previous years. Morris and [chief mechanic] Tom Anderson have really given the team the right direction. Everyone is working together and I think we now have a chance to fight for the championship.'

*Fittipaldi was on the pole with the Lola at
The Meadowlands and scored his first win with the car at
Mid-Ohio in September (right).*

Another reason for Emerson's enthusiasm about the '89 season was the fact that Patrick Racing would have a pair of new Penske PC18 chassis. 'It took a lot of work between Marlboro, Pat Patrick and Roger Penske to get the deal done,' noted Fittipaldi. 'When it happened I thought it was just fantastic for us because it was exactly what we needed.'

Roger Penske agreed to sell Patrick the two PC18s because he had already elicited a commitment from Marlboro that the cigarette giant would sponsor his team starting in 1990. Also, Patrick was a long-time business partner of Penske, and the loss of his sponsor in exchange for a couple of competitive cars seemed like a fair exchange.

In addition to having the right car and team for the new season, Fittipaldi was in prime physical and mental condition. In 1987 he had at last married Teresa, and the pair soon celebrated the arrival of a daughter, Joana. Emerson also had his teenage son from his first marriage, Jayson, living with him in Miami and was enjoying his family life like never before.

And he was in better physical condition than he had been in many years. For some time he had stuck to a regular running and work-out programme and also enjoyed a voluminous but red meat-free diet. At 42 years of age, he looked and acted much healthier than he had ten years earlier during his fading days in Formula One.

'I think it all comes together,' says Emerson of his good health. 'As long as you are doing something you enjoy, you give more of yourself. You dedicate more of yourself and you just perform better because you love the sport and like what you're doing. This is something people don't realise – how much fun you can have, enjoying racing as a sport and as a profession.'

Going into 1989, the rejuvenated Fittipaldi was thoroughly enjoying himself. 'The car is fantastic,' he bubbled after his first test of one of Patrick's new PC18s. 'With this car I know we will be able to win races and go for the championship. This year I know I have the chance to win races and go for the championship. I know I have the chance to win Indianapolis and to win the championship. I'm really excited about it. Not since I drove for McLaren in '74 have I felt so confident. If we have good luck, we can have a very good year.'

The season started on a sour note, however, when Fittipaldi crashed in practice for the season's first race on the Phoenix oval. He had been running well, challenging Penske team leader Rick Mears for pole position.

'It was my mistake,' he admitted. 'We tried to go for a more risky set-up. We put more front wing in the car and it made the car pivot around the front end and spin into the wall. I knew the car was balanced; I should have taken the car as it was and tried to find a mechanical not an aerodynamic way to improve it.'

The team had also purchased a year-old PC17 chassis from Penske and Emerson had put a lot of test miles on this car over the winter. At the time, the team's second PC18 had yet to be delivered so Fittipaldi reverted to the PC17 for the race at Phoenix (finishing fifth) and again the following weekend in the very different surroundings of Long Beach, where he was third.

Next came the month of May at Indianapolis and, by then, Patrick Racing had both PC18s ready to go. From the start of practice, Emerson was one of the fastest drivers, lapping at better than 221 mph on all but one day of the first week.

'The work the Patrick team did at Indianapolis in 1989 was just fantastic,' comments Fittipaldi. 'The car ran beautifully the whole time. From the first day of practice through to the race the combination and communication between the team and myself worked as perfectly as anything I've ever done in motor racing. We made the car work with more a racing set-up than a qualifying set-up. The whole time we were trying to make the car work well on full tanks, to make sure it was consistent through the whole race. And that paid off.'

On his four-lap qualifying run Emerson had a small problem with his pop-off valve which kept him from getting full boost. Nevertheless, he qualified on the outside of the front row beside Penske drivers Mears and Al Unser Snr. And for the race he was absolutely confident, intent on taking the lead at the start and staying ahead all the way.

Indeed, Fittipaldi made a perfect start and swept around the outside of Unser and Mears to take the lead going into the first turn. Immediately he pulled out a big gap and dominated for most of the 500 miles. In the middle of the race Fittipaldi took on a bad set of tyres which made his car understeer quite seriously, enough to lose five or six mph in lap speed. During this segment Michael Andretti charged into the lead, only to blow his engine.

After another pit stop Fittipaldi was back to his previous pace, running laps at 220 mph. Everything was looking good until his final stop – somewhere between eight

Main picture: *Al Unser Jnr runs down Emerson's Penske before taking the lead of the 1989 Indy 500 on lap 196.*
Inset: *'The touch was ... I just felt it a little bit.' In Turn Three on lap 199 Fittipaldi made the forceful manoeuvre which won him the race. Moments later, Al Unser Jnr was backwards into the wall as Emerson caught a big slide and drove home the winner.*
Photos: courtesy Autosport/Michael C. Brown

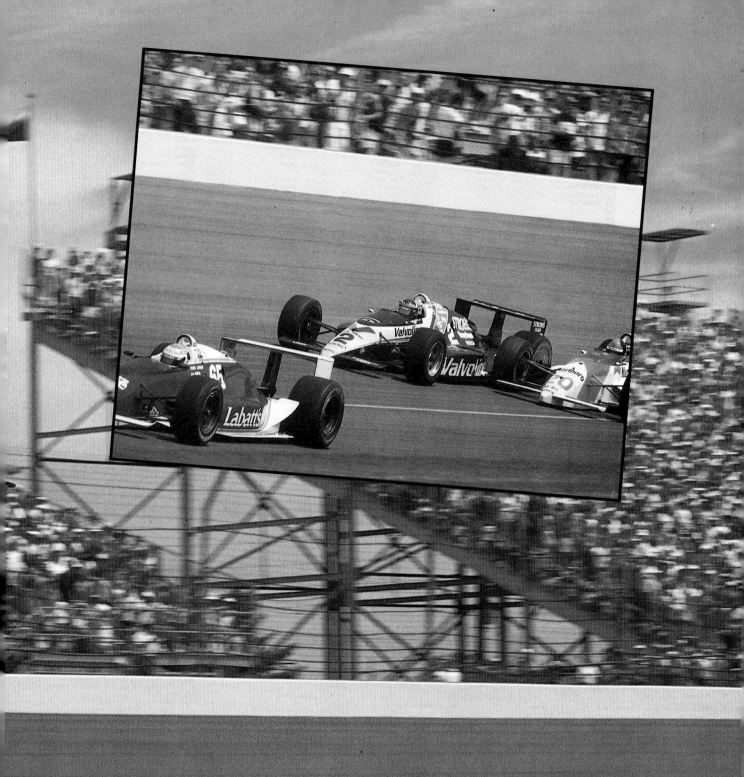

and ten stops are required to complete a 500-mile Indycar race – when he stalled. The Patrick mechanics quickly got the engine refired, but as he accelerated back onto the track Emerson sensed the car was sluggish.

What had happened was that the team had put more fuel than necessary into Fittipaldi's tank. With just 18 laps remaining a full load wasn't needed. The team had mistakenly come close to filling his tank, however, and Emerson suddenly found himself under attack from Al Unser Jnr, whose team had played its pit stop strategy to perfection.

'It was like a nightmare when I saw Al Jnr coming,' Fittipaldi tells the story. 'It was like you dream you are running and you're stuck in the same place. You know someone is going to grab you but you cannot move ahead. When he was right behind me I looked in my mirror and I could see he was much faster than me on the straight. I said to myself, "There's no way I can stop him." And he did overtake me quite easily.'

With only four of 200 laps to go Unser swept past Fittipaldi. 'That was a very dramatic moment for me. I would have been very frustrated not to have won that race. And it was like someone pushed me from behind and said, "Emerson, come on. Go for it. You can still do it."'

Going into lap 199 he saw his chance. At the first turn Al Jnr and he came upon a trio of lapped cars. The first car blocked Unser badly in Turn One and did so again in Turn Two. Unser had to change his line dramatically and get out of the throttle. Emerson pounced.

'Al Jnr came out of Turn Two much slower than I did. I slipstreamed him onto the back straight and pulled out, side by side down the straight. I saw Turn Three coming and I said to myself, "There's no way I'm going to back off. I'm going to stay on this line and take Turn Three flat out."'

'And that's what happened. I went into Turn Three flat out on the inside. Al Jnr was on the outside and there was a slower car ahead of me. In the turbulence my car slid a little too much. It slid up the track, we touched and I nearly spun. I was lucky to control the car. The touch was … I just felt it a little bit.

'I felt the touch and felt my car begin sliding, like 45 degrees! I was able to put on opposite lock and still recover. When I came out of the corner I saw the yellow and I said to myself, "Al Jnr has spun and hit the wall."

'At that moment I was concerned that he had been hurt and then, when I came around, I saw him at the side of the track in Turn Three with his thumbs up. I think

if you changed the situation and put Al Jnr on the inside and me on the outside, possibly exactly the same could have happened. You know, I was lucky to come out of it.

'In the winner's circle I had incredible feelings. I think that was one of the most emotional moments of my whole life. After so many years of racing, so many years of hard work, it was a very special bonus. It was a dream come true. There is no doubt it was the most important single win of my career. The reaction in the international press and in America was more coverage than my second World Championship. It was amazing.'

Fittipaldi's success at Indianapolis set the scene for the championship triumph which followed. On the streets of Detroit three weeks later he scored the first of three successive victories after a first-lap tangle with Mario Andretti which relegated him to the tail of the field and a second mid-race incident with the same driver. He completed his hat-trick with wins on the Portland road circuit and the Cleveland airport course, then took a pair of seconds, both from pole position, at The Meadowlands and Toronto.

In August Emerson was on the pole for the two 500-mile races at the Michigan and Pocono superspeedways. He led the opening laps of both races in much the same manner as he had led at Indianapolis, but different drivetrain failures took him out of each race.

'It was very disappointing not to finish those races,' comments Emerson. 'But it was very satisfying to beat Rick Mears to the pole in both races. He is a fantastic oval driver and has the reputation of being unbeatable on those types of tracks, so it was very special to take those poles.'

He was fourth at the Mid-Ohio road course in early September and fifth at Road America the following week. The race at Road America was difficult because daughter Juliana was taken ill at home in Miami during the weekend with a serious kidney disorder. On Friday night Emerson flew home to attend to Juliana and didn't return to Road America until Sunday morning after making sure she had safely survived the scare.

He wrapped up the PPG Cup championship two weeks later on the difficult 0.94-mile Nazareth oval, scoring his fifth win of the year. Qualifying on the outside of the front row beside championship rival Mears, he took the lead at the start and led the first half of the race before yielding to Mears's attack. But later in the race Mears left his pit a trifle too quickly, knocking down one of his pitmen and tearing apart his fuel vent hose. That resulted in a black-flag, stop-and-go penalty which allowed Fittipaldi through to win.

So it was that Emerson won both the Indianapolis 500 and the Indycar championship in the same year. His record included five wins, two seconds, one third, four poles and five other front-row starts. He also led 584 laps, more than any of his rivals. Clearly he was the dominant driver of the year and a thoroughly deserving champion.

In November, a few weeks after the close of the season, came the expected announcement that Fittipaldi would join Penske Racing for 1990. Marlboro had made the decision a year earlier to join Penske, renowned as the most successful and visible team in American motor racing. Penske was able to promise Marlboro two cars and, for 1990 at least, he would field three cars in all races, with Mears continuing in the familiar yellow Pennzoil car. By most accounts the team will become an all-Marlboro operation in 1991.

'Joining Penske Racing is a tremendous opportunity that no racing driver could resist,' commented Emerson. 'Roger's team has a fantastic record in Indycar racing and at Indianapolis. I'm really excited about the prospects.'

He started the new year with fifth place at Phoenix and a very close second to Al Unser Jnr at Long Beach. Then, at Indianapolis, Fittipaldi duelled through the first week of practice with team-mate Mears and Unser Jnr for the fastest time. In qualifying he took the pole with a new record run at 225.301 mph and once again dominated the first half of the race, leading all but seven of the first 135 laps.

Emerson then hit tyre trouble. First he blistered a rear tyre, then another tyre delaminated, apparently unable to sustain the fierce pace. Despite these problems he scraped home in third place and at Milwaukee the following weekend he finished third again, this time within two seconds of winner Unser Jnr.

A variety of mechanical and electronic problems at Detroit and Portland conspired to keep him down to seventh and ninth places respectively. Nevertheless, after six of sixteen races Emerson was tied for third place in the Indycar championship. Troubles or not, he had finished every round and remained confident of retaining his PPG Cup championship title.

'When you work with Penske,' he notes, 'you realise they are even better than you expect. I ran a really strong race at Long Beach, and at Indianapolis we had a perfect team and perfect car until the tyre troubles. The team has fantastic depth and their ability to react to problems is much better than any other.'

With his 44th birthday due in December 1990, Fittipaldi's second life as a racing driver continues in high gear. Reflecting on his 25 years of motor racing, he notes that many changes for the better have taken place in the sport.

'In the last 20 years there has been a big change in safety. When I started racing in Europe in 1969 and '70, many of the tracks were really dangerous and the cars were not safe either. I lost many good friends in racing in those days. Just to get into a racing car was a really high risk.

'I'm very pleased with some of the hard work that has happened. It took a lot of fighting, a lot of effort to improve safety and it has paid off. Motor racing is a much safer sport than it used to be. There has been fantastic improvement in the tracks, the cars and racing equipment like overalls and helmets. Today, an Indycar is just about as safe as it can be. When you sit in the cockpit you are in a safety capsule.

'All these transitions from a very high risk sport to a much safer sport help a lot with the sponsors and the public. It makes for a much nicer, more attractive sport. The odds of getting killed, of not getting to the end of the season, 20 years ago were very bad. It was very scary. It was like a war.'

Some people in Formula One criticise American racing – Indycar racing in particular – for not having the same safety standards as F1. Not surprisingly, Fittipaldi does not share this viewpoint.

'I don't agree with that. The Indycar tracks are safe and they have been improved in the last five years. A good example is Road America, which has improved a lot. There is still room to do more, but it's much safer than it used to be and they are working very hard this year on many improvements to make that track even safer.

'I like the way CART works towards safety. They are much more safety-conscious than in Europe, much more responsible in their requests to the racing tracks for improvements in safety. Bernie [Ecclestone] and other people in Formula One are always looking for ways to criticise CART and to try to reduce Indycar racing. But there is no other type of racing in the world that has a safety team like CART.

'CART's safety team reacts so quickly to any problem that it is just fantastic. CART's rescue team is incredibly quick and efficient. The safety crews in Indycar racing are trained, they're professional. They come in and get you out of the car in the best, most efficient and safe way. No other category in the world has a system or people like it.'

Another thing that Emerson takes delight in these days is the additional demands in terms of discipline and technique that oval racing places on a racing driver. 'It took me about four years of hard racing', explains Fittipaldi, 'to learn enough to be able to race really competitively on ovals. People in Europe don't realise how much effort is required and how different is the technique you must learn to be successful on ovals.

'It's much more sophisticated than people realise. There is nothing like the precision and effort required in the final tuning you must do on an oval. Any little thing you change on the four corners of the car makes a big difference in the handling and feel. The mechanics and the engineers have to be so precise in adjusting the car, much more so than at any road race.

'The whole approach on a high-speed oval like Indianapolis', he goes on, 'has to be totally different than in any other type of racing. You have to give yourself time. You have to keep in mind the first thing, that you cannot make a mistake, and the second thing, that you must be very smooth. You have to be very smooth and you have to feel what the car is doing *before* it does it!

'You only learn this through experience, through time on the race track, by working up progressively to the limit. You must work very closely with the tyre engineers, adjusting the set-up by reading the front and rear tyre temperatures. But you must always be a little ahead of what the car is going to do. You must know this, otherwise you will get into big trouble. If you don't realise the car is going to continue to oversteer, you will lose the back end and have a big accident.

'And it's not that you are just going to spin. You are almost for sure going to hit the wall very hard. To recover from a slide at the speeds we are going on a high-speed oval is almost impossible. And I think that's why the total approach to superspeedways has to be different.

'You cannot just arrive at a superspeedway and jump in the car and say, "I am going to drive fast." You have to understand and respect this very difficult procedure of working up progressively to maximum speed. When you are running lap

*Emerson says it took him four years properly to master the
art of high-speed oval track racing. At Indianapolis
(opposite) corner entry speeds approach 230 mph and on a
good lap the technique is to do each of the four virtually
unbanked, ninety-degree corners flat out without a
moment's hesitation. At contemporary 225 mph lap speeds,
the fastest cars never travel slower than 220 mph, even at
the apex of the corners. Racing in the heavy turbulence from
other cars at Indianapolis is something totally foreign to
even the most accomplished Formula One drivers.*

speeds faster than 220 mph, you have to be much more patient than at any road course anywhere in the world. You have to give yourself much more time to achieve what you think you can achieve just by jumping in the car and *going*.

'There is a *lot* to learn about setting up the car for oval tracks. It's very high precision work, very difficult. You must go through every detail, every tiny combination. The differences are very fine, very precise, and you have to feel these differences. It's much more sensitive than people realise. It's really the finest tuning you can do to any racing car in the world because the cornering speeds are so fast. Setting up a car to achieve the maximum speed at Indianapolis is the finest final tuning you can do to any racing car anywhere in the world. The more I learn, the more I love it. It's great!'

Equally demanding is the technique of driving and racing on the shorter, one-mile ovals like Phoenix and Milwaukee. Lap speeds at these tracks are in the 160 mph range and it takes barely 20 seconds to complete a single lap. It's one thing for an experienced road racer or Formula One driver to acclimatise to running alone on these furious little one-mile ovals. It's something else again to race effectively on them.

'You must drive much more aggressively on the short ovals,' comments Emerson. 'It's a much more tense type of driving than you will encounter anyplace else. You lap the short ovals in just over 20 seconds and you are under pressure all the time. It's a mixture between a road circuit-type of driving, where you must drive much more aggressively, and a superspeedway like Indianapolis, because you must be very smooth as well as aggressive. It's a very difficult combination to achieve.

'On a short oval you race much closer physically, cars against cars. You are almost touching other cars all the time, always in heavy traffic. This is something you will never experience in any kind of road racing. In all the racing I had done all over the world I had never before experienced this type of close racing in heavy traffic. And I enjoy it. I love it. I have great respect for the Indy drivers who are able to race well on ovals.'

And finally, does Fittipaldi think these days about the future and retirement?

'Well, I think the key is that you must enjoy racing and have the physical possibility to go quick. And my motivation, my love for the sport is there. I want to continue. I don't think about stopping. I have some good examples in Indycars like Mario [Andretti], who is very competitive. And he is 50. That's great! That's a real motivation to me.'

EMERSON FITTIPALDI · CAREER RECORD
(1969–JUNE 1990)
BY JOHN TAYLOR

1969

	Race	Circuit	Date	Entrant	Car	Comment
ret	Kriter Trophy–Heat 2	Zandvoort	07/04/69	Rowland Engineering	Merlyn Mk11A-Ford	*engine/Pole*
1	Formula Ford Race	Snetterton	04/05/69	Rowland Engineering	Merlyn Mk11A-Ford	*Pole/Fastest lap*
3	Les Leston FF Championship	Mondello Park	11/05/69	Rowland Engineering	Merlyn Mk11A-Ford	
2	Formula Ford Race	Brands Hatch	18/05/69	Rowland Engineering	Merlyn Mk11A-Ford	
3	Formula Ford Race	Chimay	25/05/69	Rowland Engineering	Merlyn Mk11A-Ford	*Pole*
2	European FF Championship	Vallelunga	02/06/69	Rowland Engineering	Merlyn Mk11A-Ford	
1	Les Leston FF Championship	Oulton Park	07/06/69	Rowland Engineering	Merlyn Mk11A-Ford	
4	Les Leston FF Championship	Silverstone	15/06/69	Rowland Engineering	Merlyn Mk11A-Ford	
1	Les Leston FF Championship–Heat 2	Snetterton	22/06/69	Rowland Engineering	Merlyn Mk11A-Ford	*Fastest lap*
1	Les Leston FF Championship–Final	Snetterton	22/06/69	Rowland Engineering	Merlyn Mk11A-Ford	
5	Lombank F3 Championship	Mallory Park	13/07/69	Jim Russell	Lotus 59-Holbay	
2	Lombank F3 Championship	Brands Hatch	03/08/69	Jim Russell	Lotus 59-Holbay	*Fastest lap*
1	Lombank F3 Championship	Mallory Park	10/08/69	Jim Russell	Lotus 59-Holbay	*Fastest lap*
1	Lombank F3 Championship	Brands Hatch	17/08/69	Jim Russell	Lotus 59-Holbay	*Fastest lap*
1	Guards F3 Trophy–Heat 2	Brands Hatch	01/09/69	Jim Russell	Lotus 59-Holbay	*Pole*
3	Guards F3 Trophy–Final	Brands Hatch	01/09/69	Jim Russell	Lotus 59-Holbay	*spun when 1st/Pole*
2	Reg Parnell F3 Trophy–Heat 2	Crystal Palace	12/09/69	Jim Russell	Lotus 59-Holbay	*Fastest lap*
1	Reg Parnell F3 Trophy–Final	Crystal Palace	12/09/69	Jim Russell	Lotus 59-Holbay	*Fastest lap*
1	Lombank F3 Championship	Brands Hatch	13/09/69	Jim Russell	Lotus 59-Holbay	
1	Lombank F3 Championship	Mallory Park	27/09/69	Jim Russell	Lotus 59-Holbay	*Fastest lap*
1	Coupe du Salon F3 Race	Montlhéry	04/10/69	Jim Russell	Lotus 59-Holbay	*Fastest lap*
dns	Lombank F3 Championship	Mallory Park	11/10/69	Jim Russell	Lotus 59-Holbay	*brakes in practice*
dns	Lombank F3 Championship	Brands Hatch	19/10/69	Jim Russell	Lotus 59-Holbay	*practice accident*
1	Lombank F3 Championship	Brands Hatch	08/11/69	Jim Russell	Lotus 59-Holbay	
1	W.D. & H.O. Wills F3 Trophy	Thruxton	14/11/69	Jim Russell	Lotus 59-Holbay	

1970

	Race	Circuit	Date	Entrant	Car	Comment
2	BUA FF Championship–Heat 1	Rio	01/02/70	Jim Russell	Lotus 61M-Ford	
1	BUA FF Championship–Heat 2	Rio	01/02/70	Jim Russell	Lotus 61M-Ford	
1	BUA FF Championship–Aggregate	Rio	01/02/70	Jim Russell	Lotus 61M-Ford	
8	BUA FF Championship–Heat 1	Curitiba	08/02/70	Jim Russell	Lotus 61M-Ford	*pit stop*
7	BUA FF Championship–Heat 2	Curitiba	08/02/70	Jim Russell	Lotus 61M-Ford	*pit stop*
8	BUA FF Championship–Aggregate	Curitiba	08/02/70	Jim Russell	Lotus 61M-Ford	
1	BUA FF Championship–Heat 1	Fortaleza	15/02/70	Jim Russell	Lotus 61M-Ford	
1	BUA FF Championship–Heat 2	Fortaleza	15/02/70	Jim Russell	Lotus 61M-Ford	
1	BUA FF Championship–Aggregate	Fortaleza	15/02/70	Jim Russell	Lotus 61M-Ford	
2	BUA FF Championship–Heat 1	Rio	22/02/70	Jim Russell	Lotus 61M-Ford	
2	BUA FF Championship–Heat 2	Rio	22/02/70	Jim Russell	Lotus 61M-Ford	
2	BUA FF Championship–Aggregate	Rio	22/02/70	Jim Russell	Lotus 61M-Ford	
1	BUA FF Championship–Heat 1	Interlagos	29/02/70	Jim Russell	Lotus 61M-Ford	
1	BUA FF Championship–Heat 2	Interlagos	29/02/70	Jim Russell	Lotus 61M-Ford	
1	BUA FF Championship–Aggregate	Interlagos	29/02/70	Jim Russell	Lotus 61M-Ford	
5	W. D. & H. O. Wills F2 Trophy–Heat 1	Thruxton	30/03/70	Jim Russell	Lotus 69-Cosworth FVA	
dns	W. D. & H. O. Wills F2 Trophy–Final	Thruxton	30/03/70	Jim Russell	Lotus 69-Cosworth FVA	*gearbox*
6	Deutschland F2 Trophy–Heat 1	Hockenheim	12/04/70	Jim Russell	Lotus 69-Cosworth FVA	
5	Deutschland F2 Trophy–Heat 2	Hockenheim	12/04/70	Jim Russell	Lotus 69-Cosworth FVA	
5	Deutschland F2 Trophy–Aggregate	Hockenheim	12/04/70	Jim Russell	Lotus 69-Cosworth FVA	
3	Barcelona F2 Grand Prix	Montjuich Park	26/04/70	Team Bardahl	Lotus 69-Cosworth FVA	
4	Eifelrennen F2 Race	Nürburgring	03/05/70	Team Bardahl	Lotus 69-Cosworth FVA	
4	Alcoa F2 Trophy–Heat 2	Crystal Palace	25/05/70	Team Bardahl	Lotus 69-Cosworth FVA	
3	Alcoa F2 Trophy–Final	Crystal Palace	25/05/70	Team Bardahl	Lotus 69-Cosworth FVA	
4	Rhein F2 Cup	Hockenheim	14/06/70	Team Bardahl	Lotus 69-Cosworth FVA	
ret	Rouen F2 Grand Prix–Heat 1	Rouen	28/06/70	Team Bardahl	Lotus 69-Cosworth FVA	*engine*
3	Rouen F2 Grand Prix – Final	Rouen	28/06/70	Team Bardahl	Lotus 69-Cosworth FVA	
8	BRITISH GP	Brands Hatch	18/07/70	Gold Leaf Team Lotus	Lotus 49C-Cosworth DFV	
8	Trophée de France (F2)	Paul Ricard	26/07/70	Team Bardahl	Lotus 69-Cosworth FVA	
4	GERMAN GP	Hockenheim	02/08/70	Gold Leaf Team Lotus	Lotus 49C-Cosworth DFV	
15	AUSTRIAN GP	Österreichring	16/08/70	Gold Leaf Team Lotus	Lotus 49C-Cosworth DFV	

1970 (continued)

9	Mediterranean Grand Prix–Heat 1	Enna	23/08/70	Team Bardahl	Lotus 69-Cosworth FVA	
4	Mediterranean Grand Prix–Heat 2	Enna	23/08/70	Team Bardahl	Lotus 69-Cosworth FVA	
5	Mediterranean Grand Prix–Aggregate	Enna	23/08/70	Team Bardahl	Lotus 69-Cosworth FVA	
3	Preis von Salzburg (F2)–Heat 1	Salzburgring	30/08/70	Team Bardahl	Lotus 69-Cosworth FVA	
7	Preis von Salzburg (F2)–Heat 2	Salzburgring	30/08/70	Team Bardahl	Lotus 69-Cosworth FVA	
4	Preis von Salzburg (F2)–Aggregate	Salzburgring	30/08/70	Team Bardahl	Lotus 69-Cosworth FVA	
dns	ITALIAN GP	Monza	06/09/70	Gold Leaf Team Lotus	Lotus 72C-Cosworth DFV	*withdrawn*
1	Imola F2 Grand Prix–Heat 1	Imola	27/09/70	Team Bardahl	Lotus 69-Cosworth FVA	
5	Imola F2 Grand Prix–Heat 2	Imola	27/09/70	Team Bardahl	Lotus 69-Cosworth FVA	
2	Imola F2 Grand Prix–Aggregate	Imola	27/09/70	Team Bardahl	Lotus 69-Cosworth FVA	
1	US GP	Watkins Glen	04/10/70	Gold Leaf Team Lotus	Lotus 72C-Cosworth DFV	
4	Preis von Baden Württemberg (F2)	Hockenheim	11/10/70	Team Bardahl	Lotus 69-Cosworth FVA	
ret	MEXICAN GP	Mexico City	25/10/70	Gold Leaf Team Lotus	Lotus 72C-Cosworth DFV	*engine*
4	Brazil Cup (G5/6)	Interlagos	06/12/70	Carlos Avallone	Lola T210-Cosworth FVC	*pit stop–fuel pump*
2	Brazil Cup (G5/6)	Interlagos	13/12/70	Carlos Avallone	Lola T210-Cosworth FVC	
1	Brazil Cup (G5/6)	Interlagos	22/12/70	Carlos Avallone	Lola T210-Cosworth FVC	
1	Brazil Cup (G5/6)	Interlagos	27/12/70	Carlos Avallone	Lola T210-Cosworth FVC	

1971

dns	Buenos Aires 1000 Km	Buenos Aires	10/01/71	Autodelta	Alfa Romeo T33/3	*practice accident*
ret	Buenos Aires 1000 Km	Buenos Aires	10/01/71	Alex Soler-Roig	Porsche 917	*c/d Reutemann/Soler-Roig*
10	Argentine Grand Prix–Heat 1	Buenos Aires	24/01/71	Gold Leaf Team Lotus	Lotus 72C-Cosworth DFV	*handling problems*
dns	Argentine Grand Prix–Heat 2	Buenos Aires	24/01/71	Gold Leaf Team Lotus	Lotus 72C-Cosworth DFV	*oil pressure*
1	Group 5/6 Race	Porto Alegre	31/01/71	Carlos Avallone	Lola T210-Cosworth FVC	
ret	SOUTH AFRICAN GP	Kyalami	06/03/71	Gold Leaf Team Lotus	Lotus 72C-Cosworth DFV	*engine*
ret	F1 Race of Champions	Brands Hatch	21/03/71	Gold Leaf Team Lotus	Lotus 56B-Pratt & Witney	*suspension*
ret	Questor F1 Grand Prix–Heat 1	Ontario Speedway	28/03/71	Gold Leaf Team Lotus	Lotus 72C-Cosworth DFV	*gearbox*
ret	Questor F1 Grand Prix–Heat 2	Ontario Speedway	28/03/71	Gold Leaf Team Lotus	Lotus 72C-Cosworth DFV	*gearbox*
7	Rothmans F1 International Trophy	Oulton Park	09/04/71	Gold Leaf Team Lotus	Lotus 72C-Cosworth DFV	*stopped on circuit*
ret	SPANISH GP	Montjuich Park	18/04/71	Gold Leaf Team Lotus	Lotus 72C-Cosworth DFV	*rear suspension*
ret	Pau Grand Prix (F2)	Pau	25/04/71	Team Bardahl	Lotus 69-Cosworth FVA	*rear upright*
2	Eifelrennen (F2)	Nürburgring	02/05/71	Team Bardahl	Lotus 69-Cosworth FVA	
ret	International F1 Trophy–Heat 1	Silverstone	08/05/71	Gold Leaf Team Lotus	Lotus 56B-Pratt & Witney	*suspension*
3	International F1 Trophy–Heat 2	Silverstone	08/05/71	Gold Leaf Team Lotus	Lotus 56B-Pratt & Witney	
nc	International F1 Trophy–Aggregate	Silverstone	08/05/71	Gold Leaf Team Lotus	Lotus 56B-Pratt & Witney	
1	Madrid F2 Grand Prix	Járama	16/05/71	Team Bardahl	Lotus 69-Cosworth FVA	
5	MONACO GP	Monte Carlo	23/05/71	Gold Leaf Team Lotus	Lotus 72D-Cosworth DFV	
1	Hilton Transport F2 Trophy–Heat 2	Crystal Palace	31/05/71	Team Bardahl	Lotus 69-Cosworth FVA	
1	Hilton Transport F2 Trophy–Final	Crystal Palace	31/05/71	Team Bardahl	Lotus 69-Cosworth FVA	*Fastest lap*
3	FRENCH GP	Paul Ricard	04/07/71	Gold Leaf Team Lotus	Lotus 72D-Cosworth DFV	
3	BRITISH GP	Silverstone	17/07/71	Gold Leaf Team Lotus	Lotus 72D-Cosworth DFV	
ret	Imola F2 Grand Prix–Heat 1	Imola	25/07/71	Team Bardahl	Lotus 69-Cosworth FVA	*overheating*
ret	GERMAN GP	Nürburgring	01/08/71	Gold Leaf Team Lotus	Lotus 72D-Cosworth DFV	*oil leak*
2	AUSTRIAN GP	Österreichring	15/08/71	Gold Leaf Team Lotus	Lotus 72D-Cosworth DFV	
ret	Swedish F2 Gold Cup–Heat 1	Kinekulle	22/08/71	Team Bardahl	Lotus 69-Cosworth FVA	*distributor mounting*
ret	Rothmans International F2 Trophy	Brands Hatch	30/08/71	Team Bardahl	Lotus 69-Cosworth FVA	*head gasket*
8	ITALIAN GP	Monza	05/09/71	World Wide Racing	Lotus 56B-Pratt & Witney	
2	Preis der Nationen (F5000)–Heat 1	Hockenheim	12/09/71	Gold Leaf Team Lotus	Lotus 56B-Pratt & Witney	
2	Preis der Nationen (F5000)–Heat 2	Hockenheim	12/09/71	Gold Leaf Team Lotus	Lotus 56B-Pratt & Witney	
2	Preis der Nationen (F5000)–Aggregate	Hockenheim	12/09/71	Gold Leaf Team Lotus	Lotus 56B-Pratt & Witney	
7	CANADIAN GP	Mosport Park	19/09/71	Gold Leaf Team Lotus	Lotus 72D-Cosworth DFV	
1	Albi F2 Grand Prix	Albi	26/09/71	Team Bardahl	Lotus 69-Cosworth FVA	
nc	US GP	Watkins Glen	03/10/71	Gold Leaf Team Lotus	Lotus 72D-Cosworth DFV	*pit stops–throttle problems*
1	Rome F2 Grand Prix–Heat 1	Vallelunga	10/10/71	Team Bardahl	Lotus 69-Cosworth FVA	*Fastest lap*
ret	Rome F2 Grand Prix–Heat 2	Vallelunga	10/10/71	Team Bardahl	Lotus 69-Cosworth FVA	*throttle cable*
ret	Medunina F2 Grand Prix	Vallelunga	17/10/71	Team Bardahl	Lotus 69-Cosworth FVA	*engine*
2	Rothmans F1 Victory Race	Brands Hatch	24/10/71	Gold Leaf Team Lotus	Lotus 72D-Cosworth DFV	*Fastest lap*
3	Torneio F2 Series, round 1–Heat 1	Interlagos	31/10/71	Team Bardahl	Lotus 69-Cosworth FVA	
1	Torneio F2 Series, round 1–Heat 2	Interlagos	31/10/71	Team Bardahl	Lotus 69-Cosworth FVA	*Fastest lap*
1	Torneio F2 Series, round 1–Aggregate	Interlagos	31/10/71	Team Bardahl	Lotus 69-Cosworth FVA	*Fastest lap*
1	Torneio F2 Series, round 2–Heat 1	Interlagos	07/11/71	Team Bardahl	Lotus 69-Cosworth FVA	*Pole*
1	Torneio F2 Series, round 2–Heat 2	Interlagos	07/11/71	Team Bardahl	Lotus 69-Cosworth FVA	*Pole*
1	Torneio F2 Series, round 2–Aggregate	Interlagos	07/11/71	Team Bardahl	Lotus 69-Cosworth FVA	
3	Torneio F2 Series, round 3–Heat 1	Porto Alegre	14/11/71	Team Bardahl	Lotus 69-Cosworth FVA	
1	Torneio F2 Series, round 3–Heat 2	Porto Alegre	14/11/71	Team Bardahl	Lotus 69-Cosworth FVA	
2	Torneio F2 Series, round 3–Aggregate	Porto Alegre	14/11/71	Team Bardahl	Lotus 69-Cosworth FVA	
ret	Torneio F2 Series, round 4–Heat 1	Porto Alegre	21/11/71	Team Bardahl	Lotus 69-Cosworth FVA	*engine*
nc	Torneio F2 Series, round 4–Aggregate	Porto Alegre	21/11/71	Team Bardahl	Lotus 69-Cosworth FVA	

1972

ret	ARGENTINE GP	Buenos Aires	23/01/72	John Player Team Lotus	Lotus 72D-Cosworth DFV	*rear suspension*
2	SOUTH AFRICAN GP	Kyalami	04/03/72	John Player Team Lotus	Lotus 72D-Cosworth DFV	
1	F1 Race of Champions	Brands Hatch	19/03/72	John Player Team Lotus	Lotus 72D-Cosworth DFV	*Pole/Fastest lap*
ret	Brazilian Grand Prix	Interlagos	30/03/72	John Player Team Lotus	Lotus 72D-Cosworth DFV	*suspension/Pole/Fastest lap*
1	F1 Daily Express International Trophy	Silverstone	23/04/72	John Player Team Lotus	Lotus 72D-Cosworth DFV	*Pole*
1	SPANISH GP	Járama	01/05/72	John Player Team Lotus	Lotus 72D-Cosworth DFV	
13	Pau F2 Grand Prix–Heat 2	Pau	07/05/72	Moonraker Power Yachts	Lotus 69-Cosworth BDF	
ret	Pau F2 Grand Prix–Final	Pau	07/05/72	Moonraker Power Yachts	Lotus 69-Cosworth BDF	*engine*
3	MONACO GP	Monte Carlo	14/05/72	John Player Team Lotus	Lotus 72D-Cosworth DFV	*Pole*
2	Rothmans International F1 Gold Cup	Oulton Park	29/05/72	John Player Team Lotus	Lotus 72D-Cosworth DFV	
1	BELGIAN GP	Nivelles	04/06/72	John Player Team Lotus	Lotus 72D-Cosworth DFV	*Pole*
1	Jochen Rindt F2 Trophy–Heat 1	Hockenheim	11/06/72	Moonraker Power Yachts	Lotus 69-Cosworth BDF	*Fastest lap*
1	Jochen Rindt F2 Trophy–Heat 2	Hockenheim	11/06/72	Moonraker Power Yachts	Lotus 69-Cosworth BDF	*Fastest lap*
1	Jochen Rindt F2 Trophy–Aggregate	Hockenheim	11/06/72	Moonraker Power Yachts	Lotus 69-Cosworth BDF	
1	F1 Gran Premio Republica Italiana	Vallelunga	18/06/72	John Player Team Lotus	Lotus 72D-Cosworth DFV	*Pole/Fastest lap*
1	Rouen F2 Grand Prix–Heat 1	Rouen	25/06/72	Moonraker Power Yachts	Lotus 69-Cosworth BDF	
1	Rouen F2 Grand Prix–Final	Rouen	25/06/72	Moonraker Power Yachts	Lotus 69-Cosworth BDF	
2	FRENCH GP	Clermont-Ferrand	02/07/72	John Player Team Lotus	Lotus 72D-Cosworth DFV	
1	Jochen Rindt F2 Trophy	Österreichring	09/07/72	Moonraker Power Yachts	Lotus 69-Cosworth BDF	*Fastest lap*
1	BRITISH GP	Brands Hatch	15/07/72	John Player Team Lotus	Lotus 72D-Cosworth DFV	
ret	GERMAN GP	Nürburgring	30/07/72	John Player Team Lotus	Lotus 72D-Cosworth DFV	*gearbox*
1	AUSTRIAN GP	Österreichring	13/08/72	John Player Team Lotus	Lotus 72D-Cosworth DFV	*Pole*
1	Rothmans 50,000 Race (F Libre)	Brands Hatch	28/08/72	John Player Team Lotus	Lotus 72D-Cosworth DFV	*Pole/Fastest lap*
1	ITALIAN GP	Monza	10/09/72	World Wide Racing	Lotus 72D-Cosworth DFV	
11	CANADIAN GP	Mosport Park	24/09/72	John Player Team Lotus	Lotus 72D-Cosworth DFV	*pit stop–nose cone/gearbox*
ret	Preis von Baden Württemberg (F2)	Hockenheim	01/10/72	Moonraker Power Yachts	Lotus 69-Cosworth BDF	*engine/Fastest lap*
ret	US GP	Watkins Glen	08/10/72	John Player Team Lotus	Lotus 72D-Cosworth DFV	*shockers*
ret	John Player F1 Challenge Trophy	Brands Hatch	22/10/72	John Player Team Lotus	Lotus 72D-Cosworth DFV	*oil pressure*
1	Torneio F2 Series, round 1–Heat 1	Interlagos	29/10/72	Eradin/Fittipaldi	Lotus 69-Cosworth BDF	*Fastest lap*
2	Torneio F2 Series, round 1–Heat 2	Interlagos	29/10/72	Eradin/Fittipaldi	Lotus 69-Cosworth BDF	*Pole*
1	Torneio F2 Series, round 1–Aggregate	Interlagos	29/10/72	Eradin/Fittipaldi	Lotus 69-Cosworth BDF	
2	Torneio F2 Series, round 2–Heat 1	Interlagos	05/11/72	Eradin/Fittipaldi	Lotus 69-Cosworth BDF	
3	Torneio F2 Series, round 2–Heat 2	Interlagos	05/11/72	Eradin/Fittipaldi	Lotus 69-Cosworth BDF	
2	Torneio F2 Series, round 2–Aggregate	Interlagos	05/11/72	Eradin/Fittipaldi	Lotus 69-Cosworth BDF	
3	Torneio F2 Series, round 3–Heat 1	Interlagos	12/11/72	Eradin/Fittipaldi	Lotus 69-Cosworth BDF	
ret	Torneio F2 Series, round 3–Heat 2	Interlagos	12/11/72	Eradin/Fittipaldi	Lotus 69-Cosworth BDF	*driveshaft*
nc	Torneio F2 Series, round 3–Aggregate	Interlagos	12/11/72	Eradin/Fittipaldi	Lotus 69-Cosworth BDF	

1973

1	ARGENTINE GP	Buenos Aires	28/01/73	John Player Team Lotus	Lotus 72D-Cosworth DFV	*Fastest lap*
1	BRAZILIAN GP	Interlagos	11/02/73	John Player Team Lotus	Lotus 72D-Cosworth DFV	*Fastest lap*
3	SOUTH AFRICAN GP	Kyalami	03/03/73	John Player Team Lotus	Lotus 72D-Cosworth DFV	*Fastest lap*
ret	Daily Mail F1 Race of Champions	Brands Hatch	18/03/73	John Player Team Lotus	Lotus 72D-Cosworth DFV	*fuel metering unit*
ret	Daily Express F1 International Trophy	Silverstone	08/04/73	John Player Team Lotus	Lotus 72D-Cosworth DFV	*flywheel*
1	SPANISH GP	Montjuich Park	29/04/73	John Player Team Lotus	Lotus 72E-Cosworth DFV	
3	BELGIAN GP	Zolder	20/05/73	John Player Team Lotus	Lotus 72E-Cosworth DFV	
2	MONACO GP	Monte Carlo	03/06/73	John Player Team Lotus	Lotus 72E-Cosworth DFV	*Fastest lap*
ret	GB F2 Grand Prix–Heat 1	Nivelles	10/06/73	Texaco Star Team Lotus	Lotus 74-Lotus/Novamotor	*engine*
13/ret	SWEDISH GP	Anderstorp	17/06/73	John Player Team Lotus	Lotus 72E-Cosworth DFV	*transmission*
6	Rouen F2 Grand Prix–Heat 2	Rouen	24/06/73	Texaco Star Team Lotus	Lotus 74-Lotus/Novamotor	
nc	Rouen F2 Grand Prix–Final	Rouen	24/06/73	Texaco Star Team Lotus	Lotus 74-Lotus/Novamotor	*9 laps behind*
ret	FRENCH GP	Paul Ricard	01/07/73	John Player Team Lotus	Lotus 72E-Cosworth DFV	*collision with Scheckter*
ret	Nürburgring 6 Hours	Nürburgring	08/07/73	Ford Cologne	Ford Capri RS2600	*engine/c/d Stewart*
ret	BRITISH GP	Silverstone	14/07/73	John Player Team Lotus	Lotus 72E-Cosworth DFV	*transmission*
2	Misano Adriatico F2 Race–Heat 1	Misano	22/07/73	Texaco Star Team Lotus	Lotus 74-Lotus/Novamotor	
ret	Misano Adriatico F2 Race–Heat 2	Misano	22/07/73	Texaco Star Team Lotus	Lotus 74-Lotus/Novamotor	*engine*
4	Misano Adriatico F2 Race–Aggregate	Misano	22/07/73	Texaco Star Team Lotus	Lotus 74-Lotus/Novamotor	
ret	DUTCH GP	Zandvoort	29/07/73	John Player Team Lotus	Lotus 72E-Cosworth DFV	*in pain*
6	GERMAN GP	Nürburgring	05/08/73	John Player Team Lotus	Lotus 72E-Cosworth DFV	
ret	AUSTRIAN GP	Österreichring	19/08/73	John Player Team Lotus	Lotus 72E-Cosworth DFV	*fuel pipe/Pole*
2	ITALIAN GP	Monza	09/09/73	John Player Team Lotus	Lotus 72E-Cosworth DFV	
2	CANADIAN GP	Mosport Park	23/09/73	John Player Team Lotus	Lotus 72E-Cosworth DFV	Fastest lap
6	US GP	Watkins Glen	07/10/73	John Player Team Lotus	Lotus 72E-Cosworth DFV	
ret	Int. Race of Champions 1973/74–round 1	Riverside	03/11/73	Penske Racing	Porsche Carrera	*brakes*
3	Int. Race of Champions 1973/74–round 2	Riverside	03/11/73	Penske Racing	Porsche Carrera	
3	Int. Race of Champions 1973/74–round 3	Riverside	04/11/73	Penske Racing	Porsche Carrera	*dnq for final*

At the age of 27 Emerson Fittipaldi was a double World Champion, having taken the coveted title with Lotus in 1972 (opposite) and with McLaren in 1974 (left).

1974

10	ARGENTINE GP	Buenos Aires	13/01/74	Marlboro Team Texaco	McLaren M23-Cosworth DFV	*pit stop–plugs*
1	BRAZILIAN GP	Interlagos	27/01/74	Marlboro Team Texaco	McLaren M23-Cosworth DFV	*Pole*
1	F1 Grande Premio Presidenta Medici	Brasilia	03/03/74	Marlboro Team Texaco	McLaren M23-Cosworth DFV	*Fastest lap*
3	Daily Mail F1 Race of Champions	Brands Hatch	17/03/74	Marlboro Team Texaco	McLaren M23-Cosworth DFV	
7	SOUTH AFRICAN GP	Kyalami	30/03/74	Marlboro Team Texaco	McLaren M23-Cosworth DFV	
3	SPANISH GP	Járama	28/04/74	Marlboro Team Texaco	McLaren M23-Cosworth DFV	
1	BELGIAN GP	Nivelles	12/05/74	Marlboro Team Texaco	McLaren M23-Cosworth DFV	
5	MONACO GP	Monte Carlo	26/05/74	Marlboro Team Texaco	McLaren M23-Cosworth DFV	
4	SWEDISH GP	Anderstorp	09/06/74	Marlboro Team Texaco	McLaren M23-Cosworth DFV	
6	Nürburgring Interserie Race	Nürburgring	17/06/74	Redlefsen/Willy Kauhsen	Porsche 917-10K	
2	Nürburgring Interserie Sprint	Nürburgring	17/06/74	Redlefsen/Willy Kauhsen	Porsche 917-10K	
3	DUTCH GP	Zandvoort	22/06/74	Marlboro Team Texaco	McLaren M23-Cosworth DFV	
ret	FRENCH GP	Dijon	07/07/74	Marlboro Team Texaco	McLaren M23-Cosworth DFV	*engine*
2	BRITISH GP	Brands Hatch	20/07/74	Marlboro Team Texaco	McLaren M23-Cosworth DFV	
ret	GERMAN GP	Nürburgring	04/08/74	Marlboro Team Texaco	McLaren M23-Cosworth DFV	*collision with Hulme*
ret	AUSTRIAN GP	Österreichring	18/08/74	Marlboro Team Texaco	McLaren M23-Cosworth DFV	*engine*
2	ITALIAN GP	Monza	08/09/74	Marlboro Team Texaco	McLaren M23-Cosworth DFV	
6	Int. Race of Champions 1974/75–round 1	Michigan	15/09/74	Penske Racing	Chevrolet Camaro	
1	CANADIAN GP	Mosport Park	22/09/74	Marlboro Team Texaco	McLaren M23-Cosworth DFV	*Pole*
4	US GP	Watkins Glen	06/10/74	Marlboro Team Texaco	McLaren M23-Cosworth DFV	
1	Int. Race of Champions 1974/75–round 2	Riverside	02/11/74	Penske Racing	Chevrolet Camaro	
3	Int. Race of Champions 1974/75–round 3	Riverside	03/11/74	Penske Racing	Chevrolet Camaro	

1975

1	ARGENTINE GP	Buenos Aires	12/01/75	Marlboro Team Texaco	McLaren M23-Cosworth DFV	
2	BRAZILIAN GP	Interlagos	26/01/75	Marlboro Team Texaco	McLaren M23-Cosworth DFV	
6	Int. Race of Champions 1974/75–round 4	Daytona	14/02/75	Penske Racing	Chevrolet Camaro	
nc	SOUTH AFRICAN GP	Kyalami	01/03/75	Marlboro Team Texaco	McLaren M23-Cosworth DFV	*pit stop–misfire*
5	Daily Mail F1 Race of Champions	Brands Hatch	16/03/75	Marlboro Team Texaco	McLaren M23-Cosworth DFV	
2	Daily Express F1 International Trophy	Silverstone	12/04/75	Marlboro Team Texaco	McLaren M23-Cosworth DFV	*Fastest lap*
dns	SPANISH GP	Montjuich Park	27/04/75	Marlboro Team Texaco	McLaren M23-Cosworth DFV	*withdrew in protest*
2	MONACO GP	Monte Carlo	11/05/75	Marlboro Team Texaco	McLaren M23-Cosworth DFV	
7	BELGIAN GP	Zolder	25/05/75	Marlboro Team Texaco	McLaren M23-Cosworth DFV	*brake problems*
8	SWEDISH GP	Anderstorp	08/06/75	Marlboro Team Texaco	McLaren M23-Cosworth DFV	*handling problems*
ret	DUTCH GP	Zandvoort	22/06/75	Marlboro Team Texaco	McLaren M23-Cosworth DFV	*engine*
4	FRENCH GP	Paul Ricard	06/07/75	Marlboro Team Texaco	McLaren M23-Cosworth DFV	
1	BRITISH GP	Silverstone	19/07/75	Marlboro Team Texaco	McLaren M23-Cosworth DFV	
ret	GERMAN GP	Nürburgring	03/08/75	Marlboro Team Texaco	McLaren M23-Cosworth DFV	*suspension*
9	AUSTRIAN GP	Österreichring	17/08/75	Marlboro Team Texaco	McLaren M23-Cosworth DFV	
ret	Swiss Grand Prix	Dijon	24/08/75	Marlboro Team Texaco	McLaren M23-Cosworth DFV	*clutch*
2	ITALIAN GP	Monza	07/09/75	Marlboro Team Texaco	McLaren M23-Cosworth DFV	
5	Int. Race of Champions 1975/76–round 1	Michigan	13/09/75	Penske Racing	Chevrolet Camaro	
2	US GP	Watkins Glen	07/10/75	Marlboro Team Texaco	McLaren M23-Cosworth DFV	*Fastest lap*
4	Int. Race of Champions 1975/76–round 2	Riverside	25/10/75	Penske Racing	Chevrolet Camaro	
ret	Int. Race of Champions 1975/76–round 3	Riverside	26/10/75	Penske Racing	Chevrolet Camaro	*crashed*

1976

13	BRAZILIAN GP	Interlagos	25/01/76	Copersucar Fittipaldi	Fittipaldi FD04-Cosworth DFV	*misfire*
ret	Int. Race of Champions 1975/76–round 4	Daytona	13/02/76	Penske Racing	Chevrolet Camaro	*engine*
17/ret	SOUTH AFRICAN GP	Kyalami	06/03/76	Copersucar Fittipaldi	Fittipaldi FD04-Cosworth DFV	*engine*
6	US GP WEST	Long Beach	28/03/76	Copersucar Fittipaldi	Fittipaldi FD04-Cosworth DFV	
ret	SPANISH GP	Járama	02/05/76	Copersucar Fittipaldi	Fittipaldi FD04-Cosworth DFV	*gear linkage*
dnq	BELGIAN GP	Zolder	16/05/76	Copersucar Fittipaldi	Fittipaldi FD04-Cosworth DFV	
6	MONACO GP	Monte Carlo	30/05/76	Copersucar Fittipaldi	Fittipaldi FD04-Cosworth DFV	
ret	SWEDISH GP	Anderstorp	13/06/76	Copersucar Fittipaldi	Fittipaldi FD04-Cosworth DFV	*handling*
ret	FRENCH GP	Paul Ricard	04/07/76	Copersucar Fittipaldi	Fittipaldi FD04-Cosworth DFV	*engine*
6	BRITISH GP	Brands Hatch	18/07/76	Copersucar Fittipaldi	Fittipaldi FD04-Cosworth DFV	*1st place car dsqd*
13	GERMAN GP	Nürburgring	01/08/76	Copersucar Fittipaldi	Fittipaldi FD04-Cosworth DFV	
ret	AUSTRIAN GP	Österreichring	15/08/76	Copersucar Fittipaldi	Fittipaldi FD04-Cosworth DFV	*collision with Brambilla*
ret	DUTCH GP	Zandvoort	29/08/76	Copersucar Fittipaldi	Fittipaldi FD04-Cosworth DFV	*electrics*
15	ITALIAN GP	Monza	12/09/76	Copersucar Fittipaldi	Fittipaldi FD04-Cosworth DFV	
ret	CANADIAN GP	Mosport Park	03/10/76	Copersucar Fittipaldi	Fittipaldi FD04-Cosworth DFV	*exhaust and wing*
9	US GP EAST	Watkins Glen	10/10/76	Copersucar Fittipaldi	Fittipaldi FD04-Cosworth DFV	
ret	JAPANESE GP	Mount Fuji	24/10/76	Copersucar Fittipaldi	Fittipaldi FD04-Cosworth DFV	*withdrew due weather*

By 1979 Fittipaldi's glittering reputation had become sadly tarnished. Ten years later it would be gleaming brightly again…

1977

4	ARGENTINE GP	Buenos Aires	09/01/77	Copersucar Fittipaldi	Fittipaldi FD04-Cosworth DFV	
4	BRAZILIAN GP	Interlagos	23/01/77	Copersucar Fittipaldi	Fittipaldi FD04-Cosworth DFV	
10	SOUTH AFRICAN GP	Kyalami	05/03/77	Copersucar Fittipaldi	Fittipaldi FD04-Cosworth DFV	
5	US GP WEST	Long Beach	03/04/77	Copersucar Fittipaldi	Fittipaldi FD04-Cosworth DFV	
14	SPANISH GP	Járama	08/05/77	Copersucar Fittipaldi	Fittipaldi FD04-Cosworth DFV	*vibration/overheating*
ret	MONACO GP	Monte Carlo	22/05/77	Copersucar Fittipaldi	Fittipaldi FD04-Cosworth DFV	*engine*
ret	BELGIAN GP	Zolder	05/06/77	Copersucar Fittipaldi	Fittipaldi F5-Cosworth DFV	*water in electrics*
18	SWEDISH GP	Anderstorp	19/06/77	Copersucar Fittipaldi	Fittipaldi FD04-Cosworth DFV	*handling problems*
dns				Copersucar Fittipaldi	Fittipaldi F5-Cosworth DFV	*accident in practice*
11	FRENCH GP	Dijon	03/07/77	Copersucar Fittipaldi	Fittipaldi F5-Cosworth DFV	
ret	BRITISH GP	Silverstone	16/07/77	Copersucar Fittipaldi	Fittipaldi F5-Cosworth DFV	*engine*
dnq	GERMAN GP	Hockenheim	31/07/77	Copersucar Fittipaldi	Fittipaldi F5-Cosworth DFV	
11	AUSTRIAN GP	Österreichring	14/08/77	Copersucar Fittipaldi	Fittipaldi F5-Cosworth DFV	
4	DUTCH GP	Zandvoort	28/08/77	Copersucar Fittipaldi	Fittipaldi F5-Cosworth DFV	
dnq	ITALIAN GP	Monza	11/09/77	Copersucar Fittipaldi	Fittipaldi F5-Cosworth DFV	
13	US GP EAST	Watkins Glen	02/10/77	Copersucar Fittipaldi	Fittipaldi F5-Cosworth DFV	
ret	CANADIAN GP	Mosport Park	09/10/77	Copersucar Fittipaldi	Fittipaldi F5-Cosworth DFV	*engine*

1978

9	ARGENTINE GP	Buenos Aires	15/01/78	Fittipaldi Automotive	Fittipaldi F5A-Cosworth DFV	
2	BRAZILIAN GP	Rio	29/01/78	Fittipaldi Automotive	Fittipaldi F5A-Cosworth DFV	
ret	SOUTH AFRICAN GP	Kyalami	04/03/78	Fittipaldi Automotive	Fittipaldi F5A-Cosworth DFV	*driveshaft*
2	Daily Express F1 International Trophy	Silverstone	19/03/78	Fittipaldi Automotive	Fittipaldi F5A-Cosworth DFV	*Fastest lap*
8	US GP WEST	Long Beach	02/04/78	Fittipaldi Automotive	Fittipaldi F5A-Cosworth DFV	
9	MONACO GP	Monte Carlo	07/05/78	Fittipaldi Automotive	Fittipaldi F5A-Cosworth DFV	
ret	BELGIAN GP	Zolder	21/05/78	Fittipaldi Automotive	Fittipaldi F5A-Cosworth DFV	*collision with Ickx*
ret	SPANISH GP	Járama	04/06/78	Fittipaldi Automotive	Fittipaldi F5A-Cosworth DFV	*throttle linkage*
6	SWEDISH GP	Anderstorp	17/06/78	Fittipaldi Automotive	Fittipaldi F5A-Cosworth DFV	
ret	FRENCH GP	Paul Ricard	02/07/78	Fittipaldi Automotive	Fittipaldi F5A-Cosworth DFV	*suspension*
ret	BRITISH GP	Brands Hatch	16/07/78	Fittipaldi Automotive	Fittipaldi F5A-Cosworth DFV	*engine*
4	GERMAN GP	Hockenheim	30/07/78	Fittipaldi Automotive	Fittipaldi F5A-Cosworth DFV	
4	AUSTRIAN GP	Österreichring	13/08/78	Fittipaldi Automotive	Fittipaldi F5A-Cosworth DFV	
5	DUTCH GP	Zandvoort	27/08/78	Fittipaldi Automotive	Fittipaldi F5A-Cosworth DFV	
8	ITALIAN GP	Monza	10/09/78	Fittipaldi Automotive	Fittipaldi F5A-Cosworth DFV	
5	US GP EAST	Watkins Glen	01/10/78	Fittipaldi Automotive	Fittipaldi F5A-Cosworth DFV	
ret	CANADIAN GP	Montreal	08/10/78	Fittipaldi Automotive	Fittipaldi F5A-Cosworth DFV	*collision with Stuck*

1979

6	ARGENTINE GP	Buenos Aires	21/01/79	Fittipaldi Automotive	Fittipaldi F5A-Cosworth DFV	
11	BRAZILIAN GP	Interlagos	04/02/79	Fittipaldi Automotive	Fittipaldi F5A-Cosworth DFV	
13	SOUTH AFRICAN GP	Kyalami	03/03/79	Fittipaldi Automotive	Fittipaldi F5A-Cosworth DFV	
ret	US GP WEST	Long Beach	08/04/79	Fittipaldi Automotive	Fittipaldi F5A-Cosworth DFV	*driveshaft*
11	SPANISH GP	Járama	29/04/79	Fittipaldi Automotive	Fittipaldi F5A-Cosworth DFV	
9	BELGIAN GP	Zolder	13/05/79	Fittipaldi Automotive	Fittipaldi F5A-Cosworth DFV	
3	BMW Pro Car Race	Monte Carlo	26/05/79	BMW Racing GmbH	BMW M1	
ret	MONACO GP	Monte Carlo	27/05/79	Fittipaldi Automotive	Fittipaldi F5A-Cosworth DFV	*engine*
ret	FRENCH GP	Paul Ricard	01/07/79	Fittipaldi Automotive	Fittipaldi F5A-Cosworth DFV	*engine*
ret	BRITISH GP	Silverstone	14/07/79	Fittipaldi Automotive	Fittipaldi F5A-Cosworth DFV	*engine*
ret	GERMAN GP	Hockenheim	29/07/79	Fittipaldi Automotive	Fittipaldi F6A-Cosworth DFV	*electrics*
ret	AUSTRIAN GP	Österreichring	12/08/79	Fittipaldi Automotive	Fittipaldi F6A-Cosworth DFV	*brakes*
ret	DUTCH GP	Zandvoort	26/08/79	Fittipaldi Automotive	Fittipaldi F6A-Cosworth DFV	*electrics*
8	ITALIAN GP	Monza	09/09/79	Fittipaldi Automotive	Fittipaldi F6A-Cosworth DFV	
8	CANADIAN GP	Montreal	30/09/79	Fittipaldi Automotive	Fittipaldi F6A-Cosworth DFV	
7	US GP EAST	Watkins Glen	07/10/79	Fittipaldi Automotive	Fittipaldi F6A-Cosworth DFV	

1980

nc	ARGENTINE GP	Buenos Aires	13/01/80	Skol Fittipaldi Team	Fittipaldi F7-Cosworth DFV	*pit stops*
15	BRAZILIAN GP	Interlagos	27/01/80	Skol Fittipaldi Team	Fittipaldi F7-Cosworth DFV	
8	SOUTH AFRICAN GP	Kyalami	01/03/80	Skol Fittipaldi Team	Fittipaldi F7-Cosworth DFV	
3	US GP WEST	Long Beach	30/03/80	Skol Fittipaldi Team	Fittipaldi F7-Cosworth DFV	
ret	BELGIAN GP	Zolder	04/05/80	Skol Fittipaldi Team	Fittipaldi F7-Cosworth DFV	
6	MONACO GP	Monte Carlo	18/05/80	Skol Fittipaldi Team	Fittipaldi F7-Cosworth DFV	
13/ret	FRENCH GP	Paul Ricard	29/06/80	Skol Fittipaldi Team	Fittipaldi F7-Cosworth DFV	*engine*
12	BRITISH GP	Brands Hatch	13/07/80	Skol Fittipaldi Team	Fittipaldi F8-Cosworth DFV	
ret	GERMAN GP	Hockenheim	10/08/80	Skol Fittipaldi Team	Fittipaldi F8-Cosworth DFV	*broken skirt*
11	AUSTRIAN GP	Österreichring	17/08/80	Skol Fittipaldi Team	Fittipaldi F8-Cosworth DFV	
ret	DUTCH GP	Zandvoort	31/08/80	Skol Fittipaldi Team	Fittipaldi F8-Cosworth DFV	*brakes*
ret	ITALIAN GP	Imola	14/09/80	Skol Fittipaldi Team	Fittipaldi F8-Cosworth DFV	*hit guard rail*
ret	CANADIAN GP	Montreal	28/09/80	Skol Fittipaldi Team	Fittipaldi F8-Cosworth DFV	*gearbox*
ret	US GP EAST	Watkins Glen	05/10/80	Skol Fittipaldi Team	Fittipaldi F8-Cosworth DFV	*rear suspension*

1984

ret	IMSA Budweiser Grand Prix	Miami	26/02/84	Ralph Sanchez Racing	March 83G-Chevrolet	driveshaft/Pole/c/d Garcia
5	Toyota Grand Prix	Long Beach	01/04/84	WIT Racing Promotions	March 83C-Cosworth DFX	
12	Dana Jimmy Bryan 150	Phoenix	15/04/84	WIT Racing Promotions	March 83C-Cosworth DFX	
ret	Indianapolis 500	Indianapolis	27/05/84	WIT Racing Promotions	March 83C-Cosworth DFX	oil pressure
7	Meadowlands Grand Prix	Meadowlands	01/07/84	California Cooler Racing	March 84C-Cosworth DFX	
ret	Budweiser Cleveland Grand Prix	Cleveland	08/07/84	California Cooler Racing	March 84C-Cosworth DFX	overheating
4	Escort Radar Warning 200	Mid-Ohio	02/09/84	Old Milwaukee Patrick Racing	March 84C-Cosworth DFX	
ret	Molson Indy	Sanair	09/09/84	Old Milwaukee Patrick Racing	March 84C-Cosworth DFX	accident
12	Detroit News 200	Michigan	24/09/84	Old Milwaukee Patrick Racing	March 84C-Cosworth DFX	
ret	Caesar's Palace Grand Prix	Las Vegas	11/11/84	Old Milwaukee Patrick Racing	March 84C-Cosworth DFX	accident
ret	Eastern Airlines IMSA Finale	Daytona	25/11/84	Ralph Sanchez Racing	March 85G-Buick	engine

1985

3	IMSA Lowenbrau Grand Prix	Miami	24/02/85	Ralph Sanchez Racing	March 85G-Chevrolet	c/d Garcia
2	Toyota Grand Prix	Long Beach	14/04/85	Pat Patrick Racing	March 85C-Cosworth DFX	
ret	Indianapolis 500	Indianapolis	26/05/85	Pat Patrick Racing	March 85C-Cosworth DFX	engine
8	Miller American/Rex Mays 200	Milwaukee	02/06/85	Pat Patrick Racing	March 85C-Cosworth DFX	
3	Stroh's/GI Joe's 200	Portland	16/06/85	Pat Patrick Racing	March 85C-Cosworth DFX	
2	Meadowlands Grand Prix	Meadowlands	30/06/85	Pat Patrick Racing	March 85C-Cosworth DFX	
8	Budweiser Cleveland Grand Prix	Cleveland	07/07/85	Pat Patrick Racing	March 85C-Cosworth DFX	
1	Michigan 500	Michigan	28/07/85	Pat Patrick Racing	March 85C-Cosworth DFX	
5	Provimi Veal 200	Elkhart Lake	04/08/85	Pat Patrick Racing	March 85C-Cosworth DFX	
6	Domino's Pizza 500	Pocono	18/08/85	Pat Patrick Racing	March 85C-Cosworth DFX	
8	Escort Radar Warning 200	Mid-Ohio	01/09/85	Pat Patrick Racing	March 85C-Cosworth DFX	
ret	Grand Prix Molson Indy	Sanair	08/09/85	Pat Patrick Racing	March 85C-Cosworth DFX	hit wall
13	Detroit News Grand Prix	Michigan	22/09/85	Pat Patrick Racing	March 85C-Cosworth DFX	
ret	Stroh's 300	Laguna Seca	06/10/85	Pat Patrick Racing	March 85C-Cosworth DFX	turbo
8	Dana Jimmy Bryan 150	Phoenix	13/10/85	Pat Patrick Racing	March 85C-Cosworth DFX	
ret	Beatrice Indycar Challenge	Tamiami Park	09/11/85	Pat Patrick Racing	March 85C-Cosworth DFX	collision with Andretti

1986

3	Dana 200	Phoenix	06/04/86	Pat Patrick Racing	March 86C-Cosworth DFX	
ret	Toyota Grand Prix	Long Beach	13/04/86	Pat Patrick Racing	March 86C-Cosworth DFX	wastegate
7	Indianapolis 500	Indianapolis	01/06/86	Pat Patrick Racing	March 86C-Cosworth DFX	
ret	Miller American 200	Milwaukee	08/06/86	Pat Patrick Racing	March 86C-Cosworth DFX	engine
12/ret	GI Joe's 200	Portland	15/06/86	Pat Patrick Racing	March 86C-Cosworth DFX	engine/Pole
2	Chase Grand Prix	Meadowlands	29/06/86	Pat Patrick Racing	March 86C-Cosworth DFX	
ret	Budweiser Cleveland Grand Prix	Meadowlands	06/07/86	Pat Patrick Racing	March 86C-Cosworth DFX	engine
ret	Molson Indy Toronto	Toronto	20/07/86	Pat Patrick Racing	March 86C-Cosworth DFX	gearbox/Pole
ret	Michigan 500	Michigan	02/08/86	Pat Patrick Racing	March 86C-Cosworth DFX	engine
ret	Domino's Pizza Pocono 500	Pocono	17/08/86	Pat Patrick Racing	March 86C-Cosworth DFX	lost wheel
ret	Escort Radar Warning 200	Mid-Ohio	31/08/86	Pat Patrick Racing	March 86C-Cosworth DFX	electrics
3	Molson Indy Montreal	Sanair	07/09/86	Pat Patrick Racing	March 86C-Cosworth DFX	
3	Pepsi Cola 250	Michigan	28/09/86	Pat Patrick Racing	March 86C-Cosworth DFX	
1	Race for Life 200	Elkhart Lake	04/10/86	Pat Patrick Racing	March 86C-Cosworth DFX	
7	Champion Spark Plug 300	Laguna Seca	12/10/86	Pat Patrick Racing	March 86C-Cosworth DFX	
5	Circle K Fiesta Bowl 200	Phoenix	19/10/86	Pat Patrick Racing	March 86C-Cosworth DFX	
ret	Miami Indycar Challenge 200	Tamiami Park	09/11/86	Pat Patrick Racing	March 86C-Cosworth DFX	spun off

1987

ret	IMSA Grand Prix of Miami	Miami	03/03/87	Zakspeed USA	Ford Mustang Probe	engine/c/d Guerrero
ret	Toyota Grand Prix	Long Beach	05/04/87	Patrick/Marlboro	March 87C-Chevrolet	turbo
ret	Checker 200	Phoenix	12/04/87	Patrick/Marlboro	March 87C-Chevrolet	electrics
ret	Indianapolis 500	Indianapolis	24/05/87	Patrick/Marlboro	March 87C-Chevrolet	engine
7	Miller American 200	Milwaukee	31/05/87	Patrick/Marlboro	March 87C-Chevrolet	
ret	Budweiser/GI Joe's 200	Portland	14/06/87	Patrick/Marlboro	March 87C-Chevrolet	engine
3	Chase Grand Prix	Meadowlands	28/06/87	Patrick/Marlboro	March 87C-Chevrolet	
1	Budweiser Cleveland Grand Prix	Cleveland	05/07/87	Patrick/Marlboro	March 87C-Chevrolet	
1	Molson Indy Toronto	Toronto	19/07/87	Patrick/Marlboro	March 87C-Chevrolet	
7	Marlboro 500	Michigan	02/08/87	Patrick/Marlboro	March 87C-Chevrolet	
ret	Quaker State 500	Pocono	16/08/87	Patrick/Marlboro	March 87C-Chevrolet	engine
ret	Livingwell/Provimi 200	Elkhart Lake	30/08/87	Patrick/Marlboro	March 87C-Chevrolet	out of fuel
6	Escort Radar Warning 200	Mid-Ohio	06/09/87	Patrick/Marlboro	March 87C-Chevrolet	
ret	Bosch Spark Plug Grand Prix	Nazareth	20/09/87	Patrick/Marlboro	March 87C-Chevrolet	engine
ret	Champion Spark Plug 300	Laguna Seca	11/10/87	Patrick/Marlboro	March 87C-Chevrolet	fuel injection
4/ret	Marlboro Challenge	Tamiami Park	31/10/87	Patrick/Marlboro	March 87C-Chevrolet	out of fuel
10	Nissan Indy Challenge	Tamiami Park	01/11/87	Patrick/Marlboro	March 87C-Chevrolet	

1988

ret	Checker 200	Phoenix	10/04/88	Patrick/Marlboro	March 88C-Chevrolet	*electrics*
ret	Toyota Grand Prix	Long Beach	17/04/88	Patrick/Marlboro	March 88C-Chevrolet	*fuel leak*
2	Indianapolis 500	Indianapolis	29/05/88	Patrick/Marlboro	March 88C-Chevrolet	
3	Miller High Life 200	Milwaukee	05/06/88	Patrick/Marlboro	March 88C-Chevrolet	
3	Budweiser/GI Joe's 200	Portland	19/06/88	Patrick/Marlboro	March 88C-Chevrolet	
ret	Budweiser Cleveland Grand Prix	Cleveland	03/07/88	Patrick/Marlboro	Lola T87/00-Chevrolet	*gearbox*
4	Molson Indy Toronto	Toronto	17/07/88	Patrick/Marlboro	Lola T87/00-Chevrolet	
ret	Marlboro Grand Prix	Meadowlands	24/07/88	Patrick/Marlboro	Lola T87/00-Chevrolet	*collision with Unser Jnr/Pole*
ret	Marlboro 500	Michigan	07/08/88	Patrick/Marlboro	Lola T87/00-Chevrolet	*electrics*
ret	Quaker State 500	Pocono	21/08/88	Patrick/Marlboro	Lola T87/00-Chevrolet	*oil leak*
1	Escort Radar Warning 200	Mid-Ohio	04/09/88	Patrick/Marlboro	Lola T87/00-Chevrolet	
1	Briggs & Stratton 200	Elkhart Lake	11/09/88	Patrick/Marlboro	Lola T87/00-Chevrolet	
8	Bosch Spark Plug Grand Prix	Nazareth	25/09/88	Patrick/Marlboro	Lola T87/00-Chevrolet	
ret	Champion Spark Plug 300	Laguna Seca	16/10/88	Patrick/Marlboro	Lola T87/00-Chevrolet	*gearbox*
2	Marlboro Challenge	Tamiami Park	05/11/88	Patrick/Marlboro	Lola T87/00-Chevrolet	
ret	Nissan Indy Challenge	Tamiami Park	06/11/88	Patrick/Marlboro	Lola T87/00-Chevrolet	*multiple accident*

1989

5	Autoworks 200	Phoenix	09/04/89	Patrick/Marlboro	Penske PC17-Chevrolet	
3	Toyota Grand Prix	Long Beach	16/04/89	Patrick/Marlboro	Penske PC17-Chevrolet	
1	Indianapolis 500	Indianapolis	28/05/89	Patrick/Marlboro	Penske PC18-Chevrolet	
ret	Miller High Life 200	Milwaukee	04/06/89	Patrick/Marlboro	Penske PC18-Chevrolet	*suspension*
1	Valvoline Detroit Grand Prix	Detroit	18/06/89	Patrick/Marlboro	Penske PC18-Chevrolet	
1	Budweiser GI Joe's 200	Portland	25/06/89	Patrick/Marlboro	Penske PC18-Chevrolet	
1	Budweiser Cleveland Grand Prix	Cleveland	02/07/89	Patrick/Marlboro	Penske PC18-Chevrolet	
2	Marlboro Grand Prix	Meadowlands	16/07/89	Patrick/Marlboro	Penske PC18-Chevrolet	*Pole*
2	Molson Indy Toronto	Toronto	23/07/89	Patrick/Marlboro	Penske PC18-Chevrolet	*Pole*
ret	Marlboro 500	Michigan	06/08/89	Patrick/Marlboro	Penske PC18-Chevrolet	*suspension/Pole*
ret	Quaker State 500	Pocono	20/08/89	Patrick/Marlboro	Penske PC18-Chevrolet	*suspension/Pole*
4	Red Roof Inns 500	Mid-Ohio	03/09/89	Patrick/Marlboro	Penske PC18-Chevrolet	
5	Briggs & Stratton 200	Elkhart Lake	10/09/89	Patrick/Marlboro	Penske PC18-Chevrolet	
1	Bosch Spark Plug Grand Prix	Nazareth	24/09/89	Patrick/Marlboro	Penske PC18-Chevrolet	
8	Marlboro Challenge	Laguna Seca	14/10/89	Patrick/Marlboro	Penske PC18-Chevrolet	*Pole*
5	Champion Spark Plug 300	Laguna Seca	15/10/89	Patrick/Marlboro	Penske PC18-Chevrolet	

1990

5	Autoworks 200	Phoenix	08/04/90	Penske Racing/Marlboro	Penske PC19-Chevrolet	
2	Toyota Grand Prix	Long Beach	22/04/90	Penske Racing/Marlboro	Penske PC19-Chevrolet	
10	Int. Race of Champions 1990–round 1	Talladega	06/05/90	Penske Racing	Dodge Daytona	
3	Indianapolis 500	Indianapolis	27/05/90	Penske Racing/Marlboro	Penske PC19-Chevrolet	*Pole/Fastest lap*
3	Miller Genuine Draft 200	Milwaukee	03/06/90	Penske Racing/Marlboro	Penske PC19-Chevrolet	
7	Valvoline Detroit Grand Prix	Detroit	17/06/90	Penske Racing/Marlboro	Penske PC19-Chevrolet	
9	Budweiser GI Joe's 200	Portland	24/06/90	Penske Racing/Marlboro	Penske PC19-Chevrolet	

Formula 1 World Championship positions/points

1970	10th	12
1971	6th	16
1972	1st	61
1973	2nd	55
1974	1st	55
1975	2nd	45
1976	16th=	3
1977	12th	11
1978	9th=	17
1979	21st	1
1980	14th=	5
		281

Formula 1 World Championship placings 1st – 6th + Pole + Fastest laps

1st	2nd	3rd	4th	5th	6th	Pole	Fastest lap
14	13	8	9	5	8	6	6

Note

Before coming to Europe in 1969, Emerson Fittipaldi had raced cars for three years, having also competed with karts and motor cycles prior to that. His car racing experience had mainly been in long-distance events, although he preferred shorter races. He and brother Wilson had also constructed a Porsche-engined prototype, so his ability to make racing cars work was already well proven. When he left Brazil he held 13 overall and class lap records.